P9-CCP-771

Onetime Visitor

Onetime Visitor

A Memoir with Thoughts

JACK BOLGER

Proceed with caution!
This read could change your life.

Copyright © 2008 by Jack Bolger.

Library of Congress Control Number:		2008906814
ISBN:	Hardcover	978-1-4363-5949-8
	Softcover	978-1-4363-5948-1

All rights reserved. Printed in the United States of America. No part of this publication may be reproduced, stored in a retrieval system, or transmitted in any form or by any means, electronic, mechanical, photocopying, recording, or otherwise, without the prior written permission of the author.

FIRST EDITION—

This book was printed in the United States of America.

To order additional copies of this book, contact:
Xlibris Corporation
1-888-795-4274
www.Xlibris.com
Orders@Xlibris.com
51264

Introduction

I have been relating stories to my wife and kids for years about my life as a street urchin. My wife takes it with a grain of salt, and my kids are in a state of utter disbelief. However, they tolerate my stories and me and give me enough room to coexist.

A picture of the White House hangs on my wall, signed with "Deep Appreciation from Jacqueline Kennedy", dated August 1963. I wondered for a long time if this was a grooming assignment or if it was purely coincidental, being in the right place at the right time so that some future event could occur that would have its origin from Jackie's influence on the world. Maybe it is a piece of the master plan in action!

I sat at the word processor one day, thinking it would be a good idea to explain to my kids why I am different from most fathers. Like everything else, I have put it off as something I can always do later. I am now more conscious of the clock that keeps ticking away. In addition, I think it is time to get on with it. The one big problem I have is, who wants to listen to a street kid? After many rewrites, it struck me that I was really trying to save the world and put an end to all wars. In reality, I am just thinking aloud and passing around some private thoughts for your enjoyment and contemplation.

The End of Days came and went with the dawn of the new millennium, ushering in the Age of Aquarius. The exact date of the event escapes the scientists of the world, but we are supposed to be entering a period of peace and righteousness, which prepares the way for the Second Coming. All we have to do is follow the water jug carrier, hence the name Aquarius. Once that happens, we should have a visitor according to the religious scholars. The game has already started. As 1999 came to a close, computers were supposed to crash, but we are all still getting on the bus going to work each day. The credit card bills are still reaching my mailbox, so life goes on. The story goes that we would become enlightened souls with the knowledge of the plans for the next two thousand years. Now that we have turned the corner, it almost looks like a dead end ahead. Keep the faith! You are reading a story that will ask you to consider things that are different from any of the teachings you may have experienced in your life. If you question the meaning of life, you will understand our unique place in the universe, warts and all!

God, in theory, made us all in his image and likeness; but in my case, he made the mistake of leaving out a filtering mechanism to control my thoughts and actions. Coping with life led to the development of certain defense tactics, which might prove valuable to others, and I am passing them on for your consideration.

I suppose Jesus Christ did not have a large say or a lot of choice about his rough life. I should not complain. Much like me, Christ was born in swaddling clothes. I went to Public School 15 to learn my carpentry lessons, but I have no idea where he got his training. He grew into his role and assignment. He had no academic degree to use as a way of influencing the masses, but he did have friends who were writers (Matthew, Mark, Luke, and John—no last names were needed), and they were able to find a publisher. The rest is history. He probably played marbles and had chores to do around the house, but most of that information is missing in the records. Safe to say, according to the books, he was born, then died, rose from the dead, and ascended into heaven. I have made part of the trip myself, and I can only imagine what is ahead. The historians have been unable to find his or his friends' ordination certificates, so I guess it is OK for me to emulate their actions and go forward without paper credentials. I apologize for being a little late with the new millennium information as I have been busy over the years collecting my thoughts.

We all bump into odd happenings in our lives that make interesting stories. Since I am one of a kind, who had the mold destroyed at birth, I thought I would speak up and bounce it off the masses because I do not intend to travel this road again. Moses was not met with a lot of enthusiasm when he came down from the mountains with the Ten Commandments. Still, his words of wisdom have managed to survive over time. Only time will tell if I have managed to help you with the advancement knowledge about the third millennium and the missing puzzle piece.

All my life, I have been thinking about what is wrong with the world. Why do so many people fail to get it? The big picture is staring us in the face, and we do not understand. Perhaps you have the solution in your hands! Maybe you will come across some humor in the story that will help you see that your own life is not hopeless. Perhaps close inspection and reflection of your life mirrors some of the things and same events that I have had to deal with over time.

No one ordained me to preach or sought me out for advice. I would like to share a few memories and insights gathered along the way. If I can chip in, just maybe, I have found my real purpose for being born.

Everyone has a bad day every now and then. When it happens pretty much on a regular basis, you start to wonder about your ancestors. According to my father, some kind of curse was put on the family name, which enabled him to walk out in the sunshine each day and find the big black cloud hung over his head. Sometimes, it seemed like a conspiracy fabricated just for his persecution. As luck would have it, he passed the inheritance on to his children. Years and years of the same old rotten luck and failed opportunities actually encourages you to sit down and think it through. If you think I am going to make a laundry list of the bad events that happened in my life in chronological order, you are wrong. The list would be too long, and I would come across as an old complaining grouch.

One of the problems with starting out young and growing old is the thought that it will be a continuing progression toward a final reward or a culmination of activities, hoping you will eventually become really smart or wealthy. Unfortunately, life is not like that for the average Joe. Much of life involves backtracking to various key events in your life, recalling past sins that you committed because you didn't know any better or that you refused to take responsibility for doing. There are many memories that haunt you and cry out for clarity and explanation. They continue to dominate your present life and make it difficult to put a straight lineation to events and their importance to you, the person that hides behind the mask. The face you present to the world is in a constant state of change.

1

A group of old-timers—the prophets Christ, Muhammad, Gautama, Abraham, and Guru Nanak, and a few other lesser known players—are sitting around with one big problem. They are all immortal. Day after day, they get up and find themselves stuck in a rut. They worked hard at finding eternal life and now find themselves in an unenvious situation. Bored with one another, they fight among themselves, trying to decide who is really in charge. A numen permeated the location.

"I think we should give special recognition to the prophets who have the most followers," says Jesus Christ as he displays his new robe with stripes running down the length of both arms. "Each of these stripes represents ten million people who believe in my teachings. If you count them, I've got two hundred stripes."

"I don't think this is going to work," complains Guru Nanak who is only displaying two stripes.

Muhammad appears and has an upset look on his face. "The seamstress must have been hitting the sauce again. I only have 120 stripes."

"No, that's right," says the Hindu religion representative as he recounts his seventy-five stripes. Gautama the Buddha incurs the displeasure of the group by showing up with fifty rainbow-colored stripes on his silk robe. Abraham announces his sui generis arrival with trumpet-playing assistants, with one stripe representing his ten million followers, emblazoned extra large across the back of his robe. The group greets him with laughter for helping to make the day a little brighter.

Just then, the lights blink, which is a signal the Creator's assistants give before the Big Guy makes an announcement. The Creator appears and speaks in a booming voice and says, "Looks like Guru Nanak was right. This isn't going to work. Now end this foolishness! We are starting into the new millennium, and I want things to be better. Does anyone have any new ideas for tomorrow's challenges, or is it possible to develop a syncretism among the group?"

One of the new prophets who has not earned any stripes as of yet gets the bright idea to make a puzzle. "You want to make a puzzle?" asked the Creator.

"Yes," the prophet continued. "We'll make a piece to represent each of the people you create on earth and give them a definite shape and size. Some will be fat, and some will be skinny. Their piece will only occupy one spot in the big picture. Each of them will be unique and have special talents that the others will not have. No two minds will be the same. Each person will be able to think his or her thoughts, and some will be prettier and smarter than others—just like in real life."

"But wait," says one of the elders, "that's not exactly fair to some of the puzzle pieces."

"Who said anything about fair?" asks the Creator.

2

I can define my puzzle piece by telling you about the box I sent home to my parents when I enlisted in the air force in the early 1960s. We had the draft back then, and enlisting seemed the smart thing to do at the time. Sitting around waiting for your number to be called in the draft was an interruption in the natural flow of life. I guess I was influenced by some of the advertising that was going on and decided to check with the recruiters. They talked a good story, and before I knew it, I had signed up for a four-year hitch in the air force. After my first white-knuckle plane ride on a chartered late-night flight in the middle of a lightning storm, I found myself in San Antonio, Texas, with a new identity—I along with five hundred other kids from all over the country became known as Rainbows. I think it was a derogatory term used to describe new recruits who knew nothing about military rules. Our plane arrived at about 3:30 a.m. We were told to shut up and board the bus that took us into the barren Texas prairie for a one-hour ride to our new home. Upon arrival, we were again told to shut up, sit on our footlockers, and wait for breakfast. The man in charge didn't even want to hear about the fact that I might have made a mistake about joining. After our 6:00 a.m. breakfast, we moved to a big processing center and continued for the rest of the day to say nothing. It was the first time in my life that I went without talking or sleeping for twenty-four straight hours. We spent the next two months in basic training, learning our serial number and a few other things. For example, you can't go home again until you flunk out, graduate, or leave for the good of the country. This was the first time I realized that it takes all kinds of people to make up the world. In retrospect, we did have some who flunked out for medical reasons, both physical and mental; and some actually made the "please leave" list. It is interesting to note that they were sent back to their communities and are probably living next door to us.

On the second day of training, the TI (training instructor) ordered us to send all civilian clothes home to our parents. This was done for two reasons. One, you wouldn't need them ever again; and two, they didn't want you to look like a civilian should you decide to reject their new way of life and walk away. It was permissible to keep the prayer book Mom gave me as a going-away gift, which came in handy, but all other earthly goods had to be sent back to our loving parents in a UPS box supplied by the government. Upon receipt of the box, I'm sure the parents' perspective was that after raising a child from infancy, this was all that was left, just a pair of shoes, pants, shirt, etc. No note of explanation about how I died in boot camp. You can appreciate the confusion that prevailed at my old home for the next three weeks because you can't call home when you are in boot camp. When I finally was able to make a call, my mother advised me that they were confused about the box. "Why did you have to send your clothes home?" was the lingering question.

My perspective through all this was that I did what the TI told me to do. As it turned out, I was never in any real danger following his orders, except for my brush with a rattler in Texas. Up until that part of my life, I had been a city boy and had no experience with snakes. I didn't know at the time how one incident could plant a seed of change in my puzzle piece that would stay with me for the rest of my life.

Our daily routine consisted of no talking and plenty of physical activity, running all over the huge military base in the barren prairie area of Texas. One day, a plane came over and strafed the road with make-believe machine gun fire while we were on field maneuvers. The TI told us to dive for cover in a wet, grassy ravine. When I came up for air, I was eye to eye with a five-foot rattlesnake coiled for action, sitting on the top of the ravine. Now as luck would have it, I thought I scared the life out of him, or God smote him with a massive heart attack just before my arrival. Either way, I was truly impressed by both its size and how close I came to being struck in the face during this close encounter. I think I was spared so I could be around for other fun things. In truth, a brush fire caught him while he was sunning himself on the ledge. He was a crispy dead critter when I found him, but he still left a lasting impression along with a bunch of his skin on my uniform when I accidentally brushed up against him. The captain in charge that day warned us to be on the lookout and held up a five-foot example that he had killed earlier in the morning. I don't know how many people have been that close up and personal with a rattler, but it is one ugly-looking reptile. In fact, all reptiles fall into the same category, ugly-looking hummers with funny-looking skin in colors used to camouflage and forked tongues used to seek out their prey. It seems like it is almost a way of life and fairly routine to see them down in Texas. I shrugged it off at the time and considered it a normal hazard for the area.

A few months later, after the military found out I was trainable, I was assigned to another training camp in Alabama. There, I found myself housed with a roommate who grew up in Louisiana. His idea of fun was to go out after dark and catch snakes. One night, he went out in the woods surrounding our camp, caught a brown-colored snake, and brought it back to the room in a large mayonnaise jar to show everyone. Now I was not dumb enough to let on to him that I was still in shock from the incident in Texas, so I made believe I had an extreme interest and asked for a close look at the jar. This was my defense tactic so he would not put the snake in my bed during the night. It worked, but I spent a sleepless night, expecting to find the snake on my chest the next morning. I fell asleep in class the next day.

These two incidents had significance in my life that will come into play later.

I should probably give you a bit of perspective on my early life to reveal some other defining factors. I came to the realization very early on that I did not have a big smile like my brothers. I was born with a solemn-looking puss that has stayed with me all my life. I don't light up a room when I show up. It is more like dim-the-lights time, he is here again. Having to cope with this gave rise to me trying to be a little gregarious and loud to avoid bringing doom and gloom to the party. I also tell a lot of jokes and stories, proceeding, of course, without a filter.

My early years, around age five or six, were somewhat scary. I had an aunt that caused me to hide in the closet when she arrived at my home. For some odd reason, Aunt Helen thought I reminded her of someone on television and tried to convince me that I had huge rolling eyes. "I've got a headache," was my way of explaining why I did not greet her at the door. She always made a point of pinching my cheeks and asking if I had a headache on each visit. It took years for me to feel at ease in her presence. As I look back, she turned out to be one of my favorites. She is larger than life in my memory, always teasing and always checking to see if I had a headache. I now have the same problem when I go out in public. Maybe she was right; I do have funny-looking eyes. My eye doctor told me I had the most beautiful anatomical-looking eyes he had ever seen, and it is a shame they got very old.

My nonsmiling face gave me a lot to think about as a child. I spent a lot of time reflecting on who I was and why I didn't smile like the other kids. Most of my life has been spent answering critics who ask, "Why don't you smile more often?" It gives me a great opening to describe the horror of my golf game and how it has me depressed. I can fool most people with this story, but in truth, I am just stuck with an image that I can't improve without some radical surgery. Under the mask, I am deliriously happy.

Puberty kicked in on schedule, and I remember starting to dwell on the opposite sex. I did a little thinking about it and came up with the following:

Utopia!
I look across the room and see your smiling face—
And I wonder to myself, can this be the perfect place?
Utopia, I mean, the place in your dreams—
Where life is pleasant and gay
Where you begin each day, free from worry and care—
And end it with fond memories
Every man on earth must have let his mind go astray—
To think and or ponder a while—
Well, can there be such a place.
And if there is, can it be found—
In the smile on a beautiful face?

After writing this, I had to check it out firsthand, so I spent a considerable period investigating the differences between the many pretty and odd varieties. I probably bruised a few hearts in my quest for the perfect women. However, I did not get away unscathed. I was dumped a few times and learned about the pain that accompanies relationship building. There were many close encounters along the way with special people who will remain anonymous since this is a private thing between the consenting parties.

In any event, there won't be any more poetry. However, it is possible for me to break out in song at any moment when coming into close proximity to any form of booze. It is strange to have a song inside that wants to get out, but you can't find the words. I remember telling my old mentor, "I was going to go on to pharmacy school, but I think my real purpose in life is to write a song." This has been a lifelong dream that has never happened. Instead, by age seventeen, I could read any prescription written by any doctor who couldn't write and mix and make pills, emulsions, and powders unlike the pill-counting pharmacists of today. I tried staying drunk for a week, thinking I would get inspired to write that special song, but it didn't help. All I got out of it was a desire for a quick death to stop the room from moving while I held on for relief.

I have often felt that I was born too late and missed out on Tin Pan Alley. Much of the music from the '20s and '30s had a message that was easy to understand—music that was memorable. I am a little confused about how we have arrived at the rap-music level after having had such a great beginning. I get up each day with a song in my heart and head coming from somewhere. There appears to be no rhyme or reason to the selection. Some are current hits, and on other days, they are from seventy years ago.

I have done a bit of living and raised a family of three children, and I am gradually limping toward the big trip into never-come-back land. This is a problem in that I am not ready to go. I am just starting to realize how beautiful it feels to have the sun on my face. I don't even have time to take a vacation. My life is so important that I do not know how life is going to be able to go on without me. Yeah right! We probably all get up each day, thinking how important we are, how vital we are to our little corner of the world. If you consider the number of people in the world and the fact that all of us are on some kind of special mission, you can appreciate the confusion that results from doing "your thing" at the expense of others who have different priorities. Some of us do our thing with enthusiasm while others just plod along as though time is their friend. Both are false bedfellows!

3

"I've got a great idea," says Gautama. "What if we wire the whole puzzle and make the pieces interlinked like a highway? In other words, make it like a road trip, complete with stop signs, road closures, and detours that will make it hard for them to complete their journey unless the puzzle pieces interact with and help each other."

Adversity seems to be a normal part of life, and no amount of advance planning can head off the challenges we will face as we progress toward our final rewards.

Have you ever noticed your neighbor has the same problems you have? If you are lucky enough to own a house, you *will* cut your lawn every week, in between either making tuition payments or paying your penalty for early premature distributions from your savings. Does your neighbor seem grumpy or unfriendly at times? Based upon the amount of money he owes, he will be either very quiet or very vocal. Sure, you pass the time of day over the fence when you need a break from the mowing, but do you ever wonder if he is truly OK and coping?

My childhood neighborhood was a mixture of many types of poor, hardworking people, some nice people, and others who would not give you the time of day. We did not have Monday-night football to watch on TV, but we did have a tavern on each corner, which the adults would visit on a regular basis. Some of the more dedicated fathers would just go over to get their white porcelain beer pails filled and return home while others would fight for a seat to watch the fights on the new invention called the TV and never make it home.

There were neighbors who shared their automotive-repair skills with the neighborhood kids, and this made it easy for us to distinguish between the givers and the takers. We were all in the same leaking boat, but it was inspiring to see some neighbors give a little of themselves to our future because that was all they had to give. My hat is off to those who had charity in their hearts. They had very little hope for the future, but they had a spirit that they passed on to their children. I am willing to bet their parents' lessons sustained them as they were growing up. Some of the young adults in the neighborhood also deserve mention as they would never fail to pass me a nickel when I said hello.

In my youth, we had a neighbor who worked for the post office as a letter carrier. He would send out a flyer each week and invite families to come down to his backyard and watch a movie. Each Thursday night, he set up his home projector when the sun went down. It was a rare treat for the kids in the neighborhood and a good example of sharing that has stayed with me over the years. This was my first exposure to the concept of sharing, doing something nice for someone other than you. Thanks, mister!

Apartment living brings out a completely different set of folks. There is added stress in most condominium and apartment living. There, everyone is trying to be extra careful not to make too much noise. Two complaints, and you are out! Take it from me; no one likes to move, especially my children.

You can always spot an apartment person because they go to their car to blast the radio and announce their arrival and departure with loud music. We moved into one apartment and sent a note to our neighbor announcing our arrival, name, and phone number in case of an emergency. After a year of silence, I gave up hope of ever knowing my neighbors. Must have been my *eyes*, which told them not to get too close.

East Coast apartment living is a little different from the Midwest in that identity with the block you lived on was of paramount importance. Everyone knew his or her next-door neighbor out East. This was something of a defensive position so you could keep track of who broke your window. Street stickball was an expensive sport as I remember. The equipment was cheap—mop handles for a bat and a pink rubber ball to hit. The parked cars served as the bases on both sides, and the sewer plates identified the home plate and second base. Hours of fun, but the pink ball was attracted to glass for some reason. Telling my parents that I broke another window was akin to getting a parking ticket and greeted as an unexpected expense not planned for in the budget.

4

"The puzzle people are going to screw up, I just know it. Have you seen some of those pieces? It's going to look terrible," says Muhammad.

"If we lose a piece, I'm going to be really ticked off. There is nothing worse than doing a big puzzle and then finding that a piece is missing," chimes another player.

"You can't lose a piece," says the chief scorekeeper. "If somebody has an accident or commits suicide, we'll just send in some replacement pieces made from the original DNA."

"What's DNA?" asks Abraham.

"I don't know, but the Creator has a whole vat filled with it. It has twenty-six spigots on it, and he keeps mixing it with other stuff."

We must spend a long time making many mistakes before some of the answers to life are revealed. I have reached the conclusion that births are not accidents. The Big Guy (God) grows tired of the same old players and keeps sending new replacements into the game. Life has become so much more complex that it is necessary to broaden the puzzle picture. This is a good thing because you would really be upset if all of a sudden, the newspapers proclaimed that there had been no new births during the month. It would make you sit up in your chair and ask the question, "What's going on?"

An equally disturbing event compared to no new births would be to find that there were no deaths reported in the newspaper during the month. The thought of being stuck here with brittle bones and false teeth can really wear on you. Pity the man who gains the whole world and dies before he has time to spend his fortune in a productive way through sharing his knowledge and assets.

We have a tendency to take things for granted. However, trust me, you have a reason for being. Some of us are put here just to eat the spinach that no one else wants so we don't have an unemployment problem for the farmworkers. Others are endowed with special intelligence to handle the brain surgery. The Creator also saw fit to make some people who do nothing except sit around and fight. He put most of them in Congress.

Have you ever had a chance encounter with someone in your life that affected the outcome of your life? Were they visiting angels sent to make sure that your destiny was fulfilled? I have met many people who briefly entered my life to save me from harm. Maybe that was their reason for being. It could be they never realized that they had an assignment from a greater power. What if a divine plan for everyone really exists, and we just have not identified our mission?

Regardless of your station in life or individual job or location, it is important to give it your best shot. Trust me, if you screw up, your puzzle piece will be replaced; and you will be discarded and thrown out of the game. Where you wind up is your guess. If you want to see how much of a grain of sand you really are, visit a third world country and ask the question, "Why wasn't I born here?"

While on vacation many years ago, I encountered a fish vendor in a small village carrying a fish rack home from the ocean. He appeared to be about sixty years of age, dressed in worker's clothes, but with strength built into his frame from coping with heavy work over the years. The impressive thing was that he was smiling and didn't seem to have a worry in the world. In our society, people actually cry if they don't have a date for Saturday night. Some people are so preoccupied with having fun and partying that they lose sight of the fact that there is a reason for being at their assigned location.

Life is very confusing and full of black-and-white comparisons. Shades of gray are the most disturbing events that go on in our lives. Is it OK to go to the dog track and risk a bet on a special dog, or is that a sign that you are on the road to hell? Maybe it is OK to do a little sinning every now and then because nobody is watching. Half the stress in life can be removed if we could stop looking over our shoulders for the cops. When shades of gray start to appear in your life, it is a good time to listen to the little person inside your head who says, "Don't do it." For your own benefit, it would be good to give him a name like Roscoe. He will be with you all your life, so you might as well make friends. He can also act as a great scapegoat when you want to blame someone for bad decisions that you make.

Some people are very frugal and some cheap, failing to share any of their gifts or possessions. Instead, they save everything they own, thinking that it protects them from future pitfalls; but it gives them a false sense of security. How about the guy who spends his whole life in an aloof fashion, getting an education to qualify for the title of expert or intellectual, and then dies, with all that accumulated knowledge, on the same exact day as the jail inmate who committed murder? One of the gods just fell off his chair laughing because you said, "That's not fair." Therefore, life and death are planned events, orchestrated by the gods for their enjoyment. I have decided to be bad and anger the gods a little by telling you some of the secrets I have uncovered about life.

5

"It's a game. It has to be better than sitting around counting the raindrops. We will have to have a good set of rules to follow, and I would like to propose the following four rules. One, we will be forbidden to get involved in their lives unless Father has a special need and wants to send a guardian angel to intercede and change the future. Secondly, no favoritism allowed because that would change the picture. Third, no walls will separate the races. Fourth and last, no separating the Democrats from the Republicans, so they will all be forced to work together,"
says Christ.

I was chatting with my wife the other night, and the subject of our friends' health came up. You know, as hard as we thought, we could not identify one friend that did not have some sort of problem. Getting up in the middle of the night to pee is the national pastime for us so-called seniors. Rich and well-off, along with us also-rans, have some form of health problem interfering with the golden years. It almost smacks of a conspiracy. Work hard, pay your bills, and save for retirement. They never said anything about being sick!

I made the mistake of trying to stay ahead of the rent man by moving each time the apartment lease expired. It seems it is the norm to raise the rent at the end of the lease because you are a captured soul. They forget about my two sons who can move mountains. I trained them myself, even taught them Shakespearean lines like, "Sharper than the serpent's tooth is the thankless child." Now I really have to think before I pee because I forget that I am in a new apartment and lose track of where the new toilet is located. It gives you a completely new perspective on why kids wet the bed.

I just tallied the bill for my medicine costs and found I am spending a terrible amount of money every month. In addition, you know it is my own fault. Mom warned me that smoking would stunt my growth or something. I never listened! All the signs posted along the way, and I failed to pay attention. I am paying for it now because everything costs! I can't continue to beat myself up and come out in the end as a healthy, happy senior.

Short of having a real disease with a fancy name, take a hard look at the medicines you are using to treat everyday aches and pains. You might find that it is possible to get along without them if you follow a few basic rules. Work eight hours, sleep eight hours, and have eight hours of enjoyment in your life. If you can eat three balanced meals, get a power walk in each day, and drink eight glasses of purified water, you might be able to have a new life. Of course, check with your doctor because it is not enough to listen to common sense, and we shouldn't make decisions without paying a copayment. Some medicine and drugs that you might consider going without include alcohol and cigarettes. Those that do have overwhelming diseases, and those shortchanged along the way need to hold on and wait for the get-even part of their second life. Some of us have some surprises ahead!

6

"Hey, I've got a piece that fits on three sides, but not the other," claims one of the new players. The Creator speaks, "That's because that piece is still growing and maturing, trust me. Just wait until he grows up, and you see the finished picture."

Getting back to my story, I remember the fun we had as children, playing with Aunt Annie. She was not a real aunt; it was just a convenient name to use. If you put a rock-and-roll recording on, she would sing some of her church hymns along with the music. Thinking back, she probably had Alzheimer's disease, but we were kids and did not have knowledge of that devastating disease back then.

My mother had taken Annie in at age eighty to give her a home as she had none. Annie was an orphan as a child; but she died at the end of her years, within a family setting, happy, I think. Makes it rather easy for me to understand what a great person my mom really was.

They had to open up a second sitting room at the mortuary when Mom passed on. People from her childhood attended. I have worked with many highly educated people in my lifetime, but none can compare in wisdom to this woman, who had a fifth-grade academic education and a PhD in coping.

She started her adult life at age twelve when her mother died and left her father to care for the large family of eight children. Trying to work and care for the children proved too difficult for her father, and so with tears in his eyes, the young children were sent to a church-sponsored farm to live. After two years of a living hell on the farm, Mom was able to convince her father that she could skip school, keep house, and care for her younger brothers and sisters. She was never one to complain, but her life on the farm must have been rough. She hinted that it was filled with harsh beatings and discipline. If one of the children soiled the bed, they would have their faces rubbed in the soiled sheets as punishment. It was not a healthy home environment. She kept most of the memories locked up and did not talk much about it. In any event, her early experience as a caregiver started a trend in her life as she went on to work as a nanny to four children for a wealthy family on Fishers Island in New York. They continued to honor her memory by maintaining a lifelong friendship with her well into her late seventies.

I will apportion with you a glimpse at my mom's life in Jersey City, New Jersey, the great melting pot of the nation. All streetwise kids know that you wait until Christmas Eve to buy a Christmas tree. That's when you get the best price. We always had a floor-length live tree with bubble lights and tinsel. The one and only time that I can remember my mom getting really mad centered around the Christmas tree and my father's Irish heritage.

The Irish are a very melancholy race who first, give way to visiting the grave on holidays to pay respect to those who have passed before them and second, to visit the pub afterward to rehash the event. Pop had one of his rare days off from his job on the waterfront in Hoboken and decided to visit the family grave with his brother. That was mistake number 1. Never put two Irishmen together in one place. The only way he received permission from my Dutch mother to go to the cemetery was by volunteering to pick up the Christmas tree on the way back. Mistake number 2 was arriving with a two-foot artificial tree, with a little aluminum base on the bottom. The kids started crying, and Mom really lost her composure with Dad! She didn't berate him in front of the children, but the red flush that overtook her face, and the fiery eyes, gave everyone in close proximity the message that if she had a gun in her hand, a new page in history would have been written.

Being the stubborn-headed Dutchwoman that she was, she took things in her own hands and left to save Christmas for the kids. Somewhere in this world is a man who probably still talks about this crazy woman who would not stop banging on his store window late Christmas Eve many years ago. In our town, Jackson Avenue was the place to buy your Christmas tree. Unfortunately, by nine o'clock at night, all the trees had been sold or used for firewood. Fifty-five-gallon fire-burning drums used by the merchants to keep warm lined the ten-block area. Still, it was a busy street with lots of traffic and last-minute bargain shoppers. Mom, being the resourceful person she grew into by necessity, spotted a good-sized tree in the window of one of the shops that had closed for the night but that still had its lights on. After banging on the window, Mom managed to convince the owner to sell her the tree with decorations so her children would have a Christmas tree. She lugged it home, approximately ten blocks, on the brightly lit street, past the other shoppers who thought she looked strange and who gave her an extra wide passageway. She thanked them politely with a smile, knowing inside that it didn't matter what they thought or how she looked. When she arrived from out of that cold December night, we received the gift of a fully dressed tree with bulbs and tinsel for our memorable Christmas. We had never seen a tree quite so beautiful.

Arrangements for future visits to the cemetery included one of the kids going along for safety. Here, I learned that it is OK for grown men to cry. I didn't know at the time if it was missing the person whose grave you stood on or if it was just an acceptable place to let your emotions out. It took a few losses over the years for me to realize the answer. The situation allows you to cover a multitude of problems. Afterward, it was kind of fun sitting on the bar at the saloon. When introduced to my father's drinking friends, I received a rare soda to sip. They were all in agreement that he was a great guy who would give you the shirt off his back and the last nickel in his pocket. He had very deep pockets, especially on payday!

I was always in the dark about the financial aspects of growing up. It could have been that some things went on behind my back because parents were very private in the old days and did not involve the youngsters in business matters. On the other hand, it could have been just living through the Depression years that dominated the protective instincts of the family members. Still, we seemed to survive from one paycheck to the next.

We grew up without a phone, a car, or a checkbook; and it was common for me to pay my father's union dues when I started working. The memory of my dad having to ask his son to help with household expenses was a great lesson in how life can become overwhelming for the breadwinner when the numbers do not add up at the end of the month. It would be years before I experienced the same level of responsibility for my own children. There have been many scary moments along the way. I remember trying to help my father save face by saying, "It was no problem. I'm glad to help." This is the relationship I have with my brothers, sisters, and half sister through marriage who have helped me weather a bunch of storms during my life. My hat is off to them for their generosity. However, I am still bothered by how a family seems to drift away from one another as the years go on. I think it is the introduction of the husbands and wives into the picture, which seems to alter the sibling relationships. Maybe this is a good thing in that it helps to improve the outcomes of our lives. Certainly, the mixing of different ideals and lifestyles from the other partners changes the direction of one's life.

Had I continued with my music and traveled to New Orleans as planned instead of getting married, none of my fine children would have been born. This has a multiplying effect when you consider the good things that have come about because of their birth, the grandchildren. I will let them tell their story, but I already have them pegged for how they will turn out in the end. I am just keeping it to myself. It seems to be the fair thing to do as they are still growing and making many of the same mistakes that I made as I was maturing. I marvel each time I see the home movie made of my son and his family on the New York ferryboat with the Twin Towers in the background. One week before 9/11, they were staying at ground zero on a vacation trip. I am sure each of us has a story worth telling. The history of the world changes each time we make a decision to take a trip or plan an activity during our lives.

The six children my folks went on to conceive, feed, and clothe continue to revere their lives and memory, all except my brother Michael. He died in my mom's arms at the tender age of seven and a half weeks while waiting to see a doctor at the local medical center. Mom's rewards were not of this world, but when presented her final bill for her sins against humanity, it was marked paid in full. She told me on her deathbed that she was going to see her father, and I believed her. I am grateful for having had the opportunity to tell her that her spirit and lessons would live on in the generations to follow and that she would always be with us.

I find it difficult to cast off my father as less than I would have liked him to be. For in a way, he taught me to be different. All the things that I did not like about his ways served as lessons for my future. All I had to do was go the other way. Some people find it easy to blame their surroundings and family for their current problems. However, things are not always what they seem to be. I like to think he had the wisdom to teach life's lessons by example.

My dad was born in 1899 and brought a little baggage with him. It was a sin back then for a wife to work outside the home. It reflected on the wage earner's ability to care for his family. Therefore, it was a taboo. I think he would have a hard time with two-earner households that are so prevalent in today's world. I had to learn approximately one hundred taboos from the eighteen hundreds. Oddly enough, a lot of them would find good application in today's world. However, you will have to trust me, you don't want to know. I will give you an example of what I am referring to and let you make up your own mind. It is impolite to tell a female that her slip is showing. Instead, you would say, "Charlie died." Did you get it? I didn't either.

Mom worked for a judge's wife as a maid and cleaning woman to earn enough money to make up for the money that Dad would spend every payday as he got off the bus and fell into the local bar. It was common for me to get to bed at 9:30 p.m. and be awakened at 2:00 a.m. to go find Dad. He usually made it halfway up the block from the bus stop before he gave up trying to find his way home. I never held this against him though. He gave raising six kids during the post-Depression years his best shot. Somehow, he never missed a day of work in twenty-nine years, working seven days a week on the four-to-twelve shift. He died suddenly at age sixty-five, two months before his license to work on the waterfront expired. There was no social security payoff, and his union pension that he paid into for twenty-nine years did not extend to his widow. There was an age gap of thirteen years between my parents, so at age fifty-two, my mother went out to work. She supported herself and lived independently on her own. She did manage to have a boyfriend at the age of eighty-six. He would call her from the veterans' home just to talk and reminisce.

I only started to know my dad a little in my teen years when I would stay up to have a cup of coffee and talk to him when he got in from work at 1:00 a.m. I found out that he had three years of college and could quote Shakespeare flawlessly. He was also a piano player but had to give it up when his family lost their home and had to sell the piano during the terrible Depression. After many years, my brother, sisters, and I lit up his life again. We chipped in and bought him a piano when our parents celebrated their twenty-fifth wedding anniversary. It was set up as a surprise party, and we had it delivered while the folks were out getting their pictures taken. A houseful of guests and relatives greeted them when they returned. All had a good old Irish time. Dad could not believe that the piano was his and kept asking when the rental company was coming by to pick it up. Tin Pan Alley provided many of the songs that sounded best when sung around a piano, and that was how the party went. He was a little rusty at first after not playing for thirty years, but I knew we had lit the flame. Mom's life was about to take a turn for the good.

Dad spent his final years trying to get back to his youthful love of music. He never drank after that, and Mom's extra outside work remained a secret, never discussed at the dinner table. Needless to say, I missed out on a great deal of parental guidance and also developed a pretty good intense relationship with the detention teacher in high school who offered to buy me a special alarm clock in an attempt to get me to class on time. I refused to reveal my real reason for being late so many times.

It did not occur to me as a youngster that my parents must have had dreams, just as I did, about wanting to do something big in life and becoming famous and rich. Did they reach a conclusion early on that their lives were over when the responsibilities of raising a family replaced their dreams? There was no way out of the mess. Did they dig their own hole by their actions, or was there no chance to begin with? The Depression in the thirties and early forties must have ended many dreams for our parents. However, children start their own lives and, as a rule, never look back after starting their journey.

7

The Creator speaks, "Listen up, folks, while I have you all here. Someone broke into the miracle cabinet the other night and used up this week's allotment of miracles. The miracles are only for very special cases, sort of like a slot machine that only hits after one million pulls. We want the mortals to think that there is a jackpot, but we do not want them to think that it is a slam dunk after saying a few prayers. I only use them without rhyme or reason so that the players know that it is possible. Remember that the nonintervention rules still apply and that we want the players to have a beginning and an end with no favoritism shown."

I do not ever recall making friends as a child. I was always part of the neighborhood group that played marbles or jumped over the tenement roofs in Jersey City just to see if I was eligible and qualified to hang out with the older people. The buildings in our neighborhood were set up in a long row of ten units, with six apartments stacked three high in each building. The flats were commonly known as railroad rooms, with a shared alleyway about twelve feet wide, separating each of the back ends of the buildings. The great chasm between buildings was sufficient to make you think about doing it or not doing it for about six months. Then when you finally got the nerve to make the jump, you realized that you were capable of making dumb-ass decisions that would follow you for the rest of your life.

The urge to belong, to be somebody special, was the probable motivation for trying the jump. I missed on my first attempt and was lucky enough to grab the ledge to keep from falling three stories. About thirty seconds of thought was involved in making the decision, but what amazes me is the amount of time that I have spent revisiting the event in my mind. I keep trying to imagine what it would have felt like had I fallen. It is funny how thirty seconds of your life can result in hours of replay throughout your life. The hot tar made me let go, one hand at a time, while I contemplated the fall, thinking that it wouldn't be as bad as burning my fingers off. I finally opted for not falling and cried out for help. The big kids in the neighborhood, who were encouraging me to make the jump, finally came to life and helped me get to the top of the roof.

I bet if I went back to check, my finger indentations would still be showing in the soft hot tar on the ledge. I think this is where I got the tall-height phobia, which showed up later in life. My confidence improved when I finally made the jump without incident. One of the other neighborhood kids was not as lucky. He fell, pushed off or jumped off a ten-story apartment house, and was shredded by a picket fence. He did not die from the fall; he died as he crawled away in pain into the path of a car. I do not recall all the facts of the story. All I can remember was the large bloodstain on the pavement that I had to pass on my way to school each day. It is a haunting memory. That incident had a sobering effect on the other kids in the neighborhood and resulted in fewer visits to the roof for fun and games. I think the scene left more of an impression on me because of my narrow escape. Over the years, I have thought about the other boy many times and wondered if that was his mission, "being sacrificed for the benefit of others." Consider the impact this one lost life had on his family and friends.

Therefore, the Great Spirit in the sky must have wanted me to stick around for something. The "something" is the big problem we all seem to carry with us in life. Why are we here? What is that something that we are supposed to accomplish in life? Every day, I get up to heat my coffee and watch the seconds of my life tick away. "I better get into gear and do something important, but what?" The beep goes off, and I relinquish another two minutes to history. Should I buy more coffee and just keep improvising? Is life just a big dream, or do we arrive with preprogramming for the enjoyment of the gods? If I only had a nickel for every time someone asked the question, "What do you want to be when you grow up?" I would be a rich man.

One teacher in high school was an honest person. She gave us the real facts when she told us, "Most of us would grow up to be everyday normal people who would raise a family and die." No one really understood what she was saying, and we all stayed in the clouds until later in life. I guess the arrogance of youth finally got to her, forcing her to distribute this little secret. Kids have a tendency to take possession of life much as they do with other kids' toys. They forget that they have to earn their position by paying their dues. Seeing this arrogance on a daily basis must have motivated her to action. She definitely left an unanswered question in my mind that I have carried with me over the years. If other people have already gone through her class, did her statements make a difference to the outcome of their lives? Maybe I read her the wrong way, and she was a wise teacher who forced me to think.

As it turns out, growing up in the city was a lot more dangerous than going off to serve my country. I was probably close to death five times before

I was twelve years old. Mom never found out about the roof stuff or the other city kid things we routinely did to amuse ourselves. If she had, I think her life would have been much shorter. My earliest mishap occurred as a child of eight years. I had discovered a bridge located in a park about a mile from home and became mesmerized by the heavy traffic flowing under the bridge. I soon wondered if it was possible to throw a stone onto the top of the passing trucks, being careful, of course, not to hit the windows. I kept getting better and better at it as the day wore on. As I was raising my arm to make my next throw, a horse and rider came by, and I spooked the horse. I guess he thought I was going to hit him, so he took a run at me and hit me with his chest. He had nailed me with good force, and I had to get two stitches in the back of my head at a local hospital. I have been a little strange ever since the accident, so you might want to take what I write and say with a grain of salt.

The police officer that was trying to lecture me on the dangers of throwing stones couldn't understand my logic about it being OK as long as you missed the windows. Anyway, I got my first ride in a "cherry bomb" as a reward. (We gave this name to black-and-white police cars that had one big red light on the roof.) My loving sisters, who were with me at the time, ran home and told Mom that there was an accident at the bridge and that the police had me. After returning from the hospital in the police car, I found that Mom had run ten blocks over to the wrong bridge and found no remnant of the accident. For a very short period, I thought I was special, chauffeured home in the shiny cherry bomb. However, Dad had another view about image that has stayed with me over the years. I called this lecture number 1. Never do anything that brings shame to your name or involves your father's reputation with the police!

During the late '40s and early '50s, after some of the GIs returned from World War II, extra bullets started turning up in the kids' homes. We street kids knew how to use them. We learned everything from the movies back then. It cost twenty-three cents for the Saturday-afternoon movie on Fulton Avenue, which was our only link to the areas outside of our small world. By throwing the bullets into the fire we would build to keep warm, it made the bad kids think we were strong in number and had guns to ward off any gang. Of course, they wouldn't attack. I kept edging closer to the fire to look because it seemed like it was taking forever for the bullets to explode. Hollywood forgot to add the disclaimer that real bullets hurt. Instead of it lodging in my brain, I was fortunate to have one shoot past my ear, close enough for me to hear the buzz and feel the warmth of the hot flying metal. It ricocheted off the side of the apartment building, just missing the window where the neighborhood widow sat to review and criticize our daily activities. Fortunately, she was not present that day. On another day, a few years later, she fell out of her window and died. The story went that she was cleaning the outside of her window while sitting on the window ledge, and the frame gave way from her weight.

I also had strong interests in butterflies and bees as I was growing up. I would go down to the "farms" in the lower part of the city for my collection. Kids have great imaginations, and some of the children would go down to this area for alligator hunting. V-shaped pointed spears were made from old iron picket fences. One boy never returned from his hunt as his friend mistook him for an alligator and killed him by accident. Another lost life that had a profound effect on his family and friends.

One day, I spotted the prize—a great big bee. This was no ordinary yellow jacket, but a huge black-and-yellow-striped beauty flying slowly through the area. I took it out with one shot from my plastic bat and saw it hit the ground with a thud.

Listen up as this is another great lesson to learn and pass on to your children. Never pick up dead-looking bees! The pain is like no other and is difficult to describe. An instant signal goes to your brain and advises you to faint. Everything goes white before your eyes, and you fall down. The finger feels like it has a direct connection to your brain, and both feel as if they are swelling and throbbing at the same time. It is not pretty. I remember lying around for about an hour in the park before I was able to stumble home. How close I was to death, I will never know; but it must have been close, for I was really out of it.

Later in life, I was on a field trip in Georgia when I met what I thought was a giant hybrid bee flying real slow and heavy, so slow that you would wonder how something three inches in diameter could fly on such small wings. Based on my earlier experience, I decided to let it live by hiding behind a tree and probably saved my life in the bargain 'cause it would have surely killed me. To this day, I can still remember the hum it made. It reminded me of the sound you get when you have the volume turned up high on a phonograph, and you touch the needle with your finger. I look at some of the kids doing skateboard tricks off the handrails today and think what sheltered lives they live.

For a while, I seemed caught in a near-death loop. Carrying a fey attitude around seemed a normal part of my early years. It was common during the winter months for us to pile snow high between the cars parked on the street and then use the structure as a sliding chute. I was waiting for my turn to slide across the street on the ice with the cardboard we used for a sleigh when a car came down the street. I decided to wait until he had passed, but one of my "friends" from the older guys' group decided it would be more fun to send me down the ramp at the same time the car passed.

To this day, I have never met a man as white and pale looking as the driver of that car. As I sped onto the street, I hit the side of the car and slid under the running board between the front and back tires. Whoever designed running boards on cars did me a great favor that I would like to acknowledge. I grabbed on and traveled down the street with the car while thinking about how it was going to feel when the back tire rolled over me. Fortunately, the ice on the street enabled me to slide along with the car. Finally, I gave a few raps to the side door and woke the driver from his depression of killing one of the neighborhood kids. Boy, was he relieved. For me, it was just another day in the life of a street kid.

This was my playground as a child, but it did not make any sense then, and it still does not. We just collect memories and pass them to the inactive part of our brains for some future use and go on.

I spent the next five years under cars, for I had found a completely new world. Trust me, it is possible to replace a transmission with a set of George Washington tools (open-end wrenches) and no jack. I actually thought all the skinned knuckles and bashed fingers were a badge of honor at the time. A few years later, I found out that they had box wrenches, and my life was greatly improved.

In ancient times, persecutors would put people in the arena for the lions to eat. I had a day like that when I went down to the local junkyard for the first time to get a used water pump for my 1941 Mercury. The junkyard, located about ten blocks from my home, was a big tangled mess of cars stacked five and six high in places. They didn't have safety concerns at the time, so if you entered the place, it was with the understanding that you might not get out alive. Every once in a while, one of the stacks of cars would fall and give you bad thoughts. It was getting toward closing time when I arrived, and I knew I did not want to be there after dark because dogs protected the place after hours.

It was at this point I met a monster-sized Great Dane on guard duty that day. I remember thinking he was about five or ten feet tall and all white with a few brown, spots, but to be honest, I did not stop long enough to get his true measurements. He decided I was fair game and made the great charge. I really felt like I was in the lions' den. This was not what you would consider a friendly pet. Instead, he was an angry animal stuck in a terrible assignment. I took off running like hell with the dog in hot pursuit just inches behind me. I remember trying to make my ass a smaller target by pushing it in front of my chest. When he was one foot away from supper, he ran out of chain and came to an abrupt stop. It was funny because I failed to see the chain, and it surprised me as much as it did the dog. By then, I was on top of one of the junked cars, breathing heavy.

An old man came by and offered to put the dog away if I would pay him a dime. I gladly paid the dime, thinking at the time, *Now I know what they mean when they say his life isn't worth more than a plug nickel.*

I managed to find the water pump that I needed for the car, but there was a small problem. The design of the 1941 Mercury was unique in that the casing for the water pump also served as the motor mount for the engine. In short, if you wanted to replace the pump, you had to jack up the engine and support it while removing the pump. The small problem I mentioned related to the fact that I did not have a jack that would fit under the engine. I took a damaged tree limb and had three neighbor kids sitting on the branch using all their weight to lift the engine. The old saying "Where there is a will, there is a way" never had a better application. I had to keep counting my fingers as I tried to thread the bolts.

The neighborhood advice from friends was never pay more than thirty-five dollars for a car because either the ashtrays would fill up or the mosquitoes would get to the bald tires before the car died of old age or the engine blew up. It was that bad. The state of New Jersey was close to sending me an application for a dealer's license because of the number of cars I would go through in a year's time.

My very first car was a 1940 Buick Roadmaster touring car with a chauffeur window. I was fifteen years old and a one-fourth owner with three other kids. After school, we would work at cleaning and polishing it for hours on end. The original owner said that it ran but that it needed a clutch bar. We got the clutch bar, but it never worked. We finally got the engine to start, but it started a fire under the hood. Our first instinct was to run, but one of us snuffed the fire out by throwing a large towel over the flames. The owner of the gas station, where we had it parked, got a little nervous after the incident and told us we would have to move it. That presented a small problem in that none of us was old enough to buy license plates. We finally had to call the junkyard that gave us twelve dollars and towed it away.

Months later, we saw this beautiful copy of our car at the shopping center. It looked brand new; and the owner told us he bought it for $200 from the junkyard, had it painted black, and put in a new clutch bar because the one that was in it was too small to engage the clutch. After this lesson and going on to install two engines, four transmissions, and one rear end, I felt the confidence I needed to face the world; and so I moved on.

Actually, I gave away a nice set of wrenches at the time, vowing to never use them again. It seems I made a bad mistake when I was helping a friend (older bigger guy) install a new rear end in his car. We were so happy to have pulled this off with the help of a bumper jack that in our rush to try it out, it seems I forgot to tighten the lug nuts on the back wheel! Two blocks later, during the test drive, the tire came off along with the back fender. I'm not saying this was get-even time for all the persecution that the big kids inflicted on us little kids. My defense that I thought the other guy tightened the lug nuts seemed to hold up in cross-examination.

On my eighteenth birthday, the ashtrays were full in my 1940 Chevy Coupe, so I bought what I thought was my first real upgrade in a car. I broke the rules and paid $100 for a 1953 Kaiser. My friends from the neighborhood joined in the gas collection, and we all took off for a swim in the ocean down at the Jersey Shore. On the way back, right at the top of the Edison Bridge, one of the pistons tore a hole through the engine block, causing the engine to die. Being the resourceful offspring of my mother, I took the car out of gear and coasted down the steep bridge into a bowling alley parking lot. We could not leave it sitting on private property, so my friends and I removed the license plates and proceeded to stone it for being bad. Months later, the state police called me to ask if I still wanted it. I said, "No, sir," and the police junked it for its scrap value.

My next venture was to buy half a car. Everything from the driver's door back was perfect, but the front of the car was missing. The price was right, and I knew up front that the car had been in an accident. No problem, back I went to the junkyard and purchased a used engine, along with a hood, grill, and two fenders. Installation was a snap with the box wrenches, but I forgot one thing. The engine I bought was from fifteen years earlier. I think I should have also replaced the transmission because it was the slowest car I had ever driven. Something was wrong! Oddly enough, the bolts matched up, but I got what I paid for. I tried to pass a bus and lost the drag race. After that, my friends were reluctant to chip in for gas money because there was no thrill in riding in such a slow car. "This might be a clue to a long life for teenagers. Buy them a slow car!"

A year later, I asked a friend if I could use his car to make a trip to Annapolis, Maryland, to attend a christening with my mother and sister. On the way back, the spring that controlled the gas pedal snapped and went to the floor, causing the car to come to an abrupt halt. I was on the open road between towns in a farming area, and the area was pretty devoid of gas stations. I pulled over and started to walk to a repair shop when a huge rottweiler spotted me trying to walk by his farm *without his permission*. He was fast and coming in a full charge down the hillside, barking his head off. The only thing I could think of doing was to run across three lanes of heavy traffic to get away from him and invite another close encounter with the Grim Reaper. The dog, trained not to play in traffic, stopped before venturing onto the highway. The farmer came out to see what all the commotion was about and called the dog off just in time. My mom and sis finally stopped screaming and waited in the car while I went on my mission.

I then spoke with a mechanic at a garage up the road and was informed that it might be two days before he could find a replacement part. I explained that I had a total of fifteen dollars in my pocket that I was trying to save for my funeral since I had to go back for the car, and I did not know where the dog was. He found this funny and helped me rig a long stiff wire directly to the carburetor through the floorboard. He didn't think it would work, but I explained that instead of pushing down on the gas pedal, I could pull up on the wire when I needed to go forward.

I made the remaining two-hundred-mile trip pulling on the wire. My arm was so sore and swollen when we arrived, I could hardly move it. I made it home and still had ten bucks to buy the spring-loaded gas pedal at the junkyard the next day. By now, the Great Dane just barked at me when I visited his junkyard. He must have a good memory of what happened when he reached the end of his chain. I guess you learn as you go along! To my sharing mechanic friend who allowed me to continue on my road to destiny, I can only say, "Thanks, mister."

I find it sad that people cover up the problems they have with their cars and sell them to unsuspecting people, thinking that "Let the buyer beware" is the correct way to live their lives. "Revenge is mine," said the Lord. It is all about sharing by absorbing our own misfortunes instead of passing them on. Remember, you have an interview to go on, and the Almighty is a fun-seeking person.

8

*The Creator looks over and sees Guru Nanak playing with an odd-shaped box.
"What have you got there?" he asks.*

"These are dart bombs," replies Guru Nanak.

"What do you use them for?"

*"Well, a guy has to have some fun, and these are designed to fire warning
shots at some of the players when they are deviating off the road. Life for these
puzzle pieces will be so confusing that they will get lost and lose direction. Their
real name is shit darts. When I hit someone with one, it causes him or her to
pause and think. That way, they will not suspect us for being responsible. They
just figure it happens by accident."*

*"OK," says the Creator, "but let's be careful not to give too many out because
the guys around here are bored silly. By the way, are you the one who has been
harassing Bolger all these years with your target practice? He mentions it in his
nightly prayers and wants it to stop."*

The place where you grow up influences what you consider normal. When
a new kid showed up in the neighborhood and talked of things, which were
different, our thoughts turned to new adventures that might be ahead.

We had one such boy who was a little older and talked about the power
of the gang. This is a city thing that I think all young boys hear about as
they are growing up and are intrigued to be on the inside of and part of
the happening group. He actively recruited me and another kid to join
his gang. Two days later, we had to participate in a gang war at a certain
location. I remember the feeling of thinking we were going off to fight like
the GIs. I recall not feeling any fear, for we were just dumb, stupid kids on
a mission. I must have developed an attitude from watching the war movies
in the '40s.

We showed up as a gang of three, and the seventy-five members of the
other gang who showed up were relieved to find that they only had to make
a show of force with their studded belts and baseball bats. The leader of my
gang started to cry when punched by the leader of the other gang. I never

managed to develop tenure with the group after that as I had lost faith in the leader and drifted toward new things. Thank God we did not win and have to go down in history as heroes. Present gang members should take note that they are going through a very brief period of their lives and that it doesn't matter if they belong. The sad part is the garbage you will have to carry with you for the rest of your life because of the bad memories you will collect.

We had a kid from New York City show up at school one year, but he did not last long. He pulled a gun on me in the toolroom of the carpentry class and told me to give him some of the tools that were off-limits. We had a sign-out procedure for all tools and accounted for them at the end of class. I announced in a loud voice that he could have anything he wanted as long as he had a gun. The teacher, whose only reason for living may have been to save me, overheard the conversation and rushed the kid to the ground. Thanks, mister!

Strange as it may seem, I received no special counseling for my trauma at the time. It seems like it is an automatic reflex action to release all the shrinks on the populous whenever something bad happens. I guess we have educated too many people, and we have extra psychology majors lurking around the corners. I just shrugged off the incident and went on with my wood project.

I realized very early on that the only way I was going to escape poverty in the city was to get rich. Around about age ten or eleven, I began to find small jobs. I started getting an hour of work here and there, helping the local merchants. I had as many as five jobs at the same time and attended school. I would put the paper sections together at the candy store and receive ice-cream sodas in payment for my efforts. After a while, I started to put on a lot of weight and developed the biggest set of knockers in the area. I had the girls in the neighborhood beat by a mile. I took a lot of ribbing from the big guys who thought it was fun to cop a feel. Ethics and concern for the feelings of others was always missing in our streets.

Next door was a laundry, and they always needed their floors swept or some clothes folded or a machine fixed. This was the place where I learned everything you could ever want to know about electricity. I tried to fix a washing machine solenoid switch on the advice of the store owner who told me to rub some graphite grease on the shaft. This action on my part introduced me to the almighty power of 220 volts. After picking myself up from the floor on the other side of the room, the owner told me to make sure I turn the power off before working on the machines. That was just a minor point that he took for granted or conveniently forgot to tell me about.

A quarter here and a dime there was more money than I had ever seen, so I continued to go back for more lessons. This was also the place where they gave me a personal workout gym in the form of a three-wheeled bicycle. Picture a large container about the size of a washing machine mounted on the front end of a bicycle with two front wheels. This was my constant companion for about a year. I wore out a few sets of brakes going down the hills because the bike was so fast and top-heavy. Coming up the hills was another story. I developed into a strong little kid, pushing the bike full of laundry up the steep, sloping streets. When I was not helping to make laundry or linoleum deliveries, I would wash the cars for the merchants. I always kept myself employed throughout high school. It made me a better person having responsibility at an early age. It stretched me for the things coming later in life.

One of the least rewarding jobs I had was setting up pins in the local bowling alley. This was before the days of the automatic pin machines. My hands were a little small at the time, and it was difficult to get all the pins set up in a timely fashion. The score sheets the bowlers used were designed a little different then the current models. I think you recorded ten extra points if you nailed a pinsetter.

The proper way to set pins was to clear the ball first, step on the pedal that would force the pin spots to appear, steady the pins in the proper spot, release the pedal, then make it back to the sitting ledge, and pull your legs up before ten hard wooden pins came flying your way. I did not have good coordination, and black-and-blue spots were common on my torso. I began to try to get an edge by delaying the ball return to try to buy some extra time, but the bowlers would have none of that. They grabbed me one day and used me to shine the alley with my bottom. The edge on the alley, where errant balls go into the gutter, developed splinters that pierced my pants and left leg. The blood flowing out of my leg scared the hell out of the big guys, who were using me as a mop. They all agreed however that there was no need to call an ambulance since they could do any necessary surgery using the switchblade they had in their pockets. At least, they went to the movies and learned that you use your trusty lighter to sterilize the blade before using it for surgery. It hurt like hell for a long while because they only got some of the splinter material from my leg. After that, my relationship with them improved, especially when they found out that I did not tell my parents about the incident.

Some of the best advice I can pass on to you is never apply for a plumber's helper job. I made this mistake at age sixteen. Part of the fun of this job involved taking a bus and the subway to get to Manhattan and meeting the plumber at a different location each day. He specialized in making repairs at the big hotels in New York City. My job was to crawl through the walls twenty feet or so from the entrance on my belly and lead the new pipe into the fittings. I met many rats on this assignment. Traveling home each night was fun in that I never had a problem getting a seat on the train or bus.

With a little more involvement from my parents, I probably could have avoided a lot of the street influence that dominated my early years, but it is just history at this point. Everything in life costs something, and that rule holds true for your parents. Those were tough times that my parents spent keeping a roof over my head, so I cannot fault them. Even at this late stage of my life, I can say that I truly loved them.

With some of my hard-earned money, I rented my first musical instrument, a clarinet that had a price tag of $7 a month. During one of my lean months, I could not afford the rental, so I took it back to the store owner. He was so impressed that he did not have to go chase me to return it that he offered me a job. This had never happened to him before, and I guess he was impressed. Thanks, mister!

I never really had the time to practice because I was always working. However, I stayed with it over the years; and while I never aspired to perform, it has brought me a great deal of enjoyment. Not being a visual person made it difficult to read the notes, and I lost interest. Recorded music turned out to be the solution. I was inspired to try to duplicate the notes listening to Benny Goodman and trying to play along. He was a great teacher!

I met some sharing friends during my teen years. One was a trombone player and well-known in New Jersey. He stayed with his craft and provided entertainment to the masses. He was the one who allowed me to borrow his car for my famous trip to Annapolis. I am grateful to his family who allowed us to practice after school at their home. His brother was a clarinet player who served as a mentor during my early years. Both were good friends who occupied my quiet time.

It takes a long time to reach the level you need to be at to perform in public, so I developed a great respect for good musicians along the way. A gift of a used clarinet from a family friend improved my training. It was a much better unit than the one I had, and it made the journey a lot easier. Again, I wish to say thanks, for I still play it today.

I passed on the favor later in life by giving a young student a trombone that I had acquired at a garage sale. My music training suffered a setback in the air force, but I picked it up again later in technical training school. My snake-friend roommate wanted to play the trumpet, so I took him down to a local pawnshop and got him started on a used instrument. Between the two of us, we managed to lose many of our barrack friends because frankly, it was hard on the ears.

This is about the time in my life where I start to look at life a little differently. In the '60s, visiting the state of Alabama turned out to be an education in hatred. When we arrived at Gunter Air Force Base, the commander at the base advised all the troops that if we had any Negro friends, we were to say goodbye to them at the gate, and advised not to travel into town together. I shared my early years with classmates who were black and enjoyed many good times together. I thought the commander was wrong about this advice, but I followed the rules and went to the town of Montgomery by myself. I made the mistake of walking in front of a tavern frequented by Negro workers. About thirty black men came running out of the tavern to see what a white dude was doing on their side of the street. A large moan went up in the crowd, and my heart stopped beating while I watched my short life passing in front of me. No one had told me that the white people had sidewalks, and the black people had to walk on the dirt. Add in the nasty signs in the stores that said Whites Only, and it was like returning to nineteen hundreds New York when Irish Not Welcome signs were prevalent. Sixty years went by, and people are still stupid. We have laws on the books against cruelty toward animals; but our legacy for the twentieth century is prejudice, hatred, and pain for our fellow man and neighbors. Why? How much better would it have been if the men had greeted me and broke the chains that bind them with hatred? Not to worry, it all comes out even in the end.

9

I can't get over how the gods have fun giving me narrow escapes. It must be part of their overall training mission. On this occasion, I only thought I died. I had a strong interest in good big band music and liked to play it loud on the car radio, much like the kids of today. I was also a collector of tall junked old console radios that you would find on the trash pile on garbage day. My mom said, "It is a sin to throw away good things," so I went about recovering all the old vacuum tubes and twelve-inch woofer speakers I could find. I got the idea of mounting one of the big speakers in the back window of one of my cars and having a fun time with my music.

One day, I pulled into work and forgot to turn the radio off after listening to a big band song at full volume. The ignition switch killed the radio, and I gave it no further thought. I was working the four-to-twelve shifts at the time. Back in those days, the car radio had to warm up before it would work. I managed to get about thirty-five feet out of the lonely dark parking lot before a really loud version of the opening score from *Jaws* greeted me from the depths of the dark backseat. Talk about leaving stains. My mother taught me to wear clean underwear, but this was a special situation I will always remember!

Back in the fifties, we were not latchkey kids. It was normal to hang out on the street until suppertime. I got smart along the way and took a raw potato to school with me. *Cold* was the word used to describe us street urchins, not *cool*. The afternoon bonfire was something you really looked forward to down at the vacant lot during the freezing winters. Putting a potatoe (I spelled this wrong intentionally so everyone would understand) in the fire was my answer to the afternoon snack problem. At least, I was making progress, learning to use the fire for good things instead of setting off bullets. I always volunteer to cook when I attend these newfangled afternoon barbeques. It gives me time to reflect back and do some more time traveling.

It is funny how minor, little things turn out to be related to future events. When I was hanging around the linoleum and carpet store, I would get to go with the carpet installers and help stretch the carpet. They did not trust me to make a cut in the carpet, but I was qualified to do the heavy work. I was working with a Hungarian fellow who had managed to grow to the ripe age of forty without ever having received an electrical shock. One day, while we were working together, he was sweating a lot and touched a metal radiator with his cutting knife and at the same time brushed against a wall socket. Talk about confusion; he couldn't understand what was happening to him even after he did it twice. With me not speaking Hungarian, it was quite a scene. He kept dancing around the room, yelling about the spirits that were invading his body.

Not enough silver spoons were available to pass around my neighborhood. I sometimes think the gods get a kick out of watching us spoonless puzzle pieces work. It seems I spent my whole childhood at work. My teachers in grammar school saw something in me and identified me as "most likely to succeed." This surprised me at the time, but I have always felt most comfortable when I am doing hard work. I was always looking for the shine that I get from sticking to a task and seeing it through, no matter how difficult the job.

10

Time travel is so easy when you want to go backward. Revisiting the past is very beneficial because there is a lot of history out there that is helpful in making decisions. Possibly, the reason the young screw up so often is the fact that they do not have any reference points to draw from. I know it sounds old-fashioned to say listen to your elders, but it's great advice.

I was helping my son move his family into their new home, and I was amazed to see that my grandsons had a pair of shoes for each day of the week. Back I went to the memory of my relationship with my brothers. My older brother by two years always got first crack at the used shoes our mom collected from somewhere. I was second after him, but he was good at wearing them out, so I used the repaired model. Thick cardboard was a great collectible that served the purpose of covering the big holes in the shoes and was near and dear to my feet for many years.

I bought my first pair of new shoes with my first real paycheck, and boy, did they hurt. Who knew? I never realized that Mom was doing me a favor all those years!

By the way, I had two each of the best brothers and sisters a person can have. They all somehow survived by living what they learned as street kids. I am particularly thankful to my older brother who was my protector when the big kids in the neighborhood stepped out of line.

My siblings inherited many of my mother's traits, namely hard work and dedication to their wives and husbands and any task. They received the same in-depth training that I received, and it showed.

Since I have to respect their privacy, this story is about my thoughts, not of my siblings, children, wife, and friends. They do not embrace my strange beliefs or theories about life, and I am intentionally leaving it to them to tell their own stories. Somewhere along the way, I made a bad turn or something that changed my life and made me very different from others. I never seem to smile for some reason!

11

Cleaning out has always been a problem for me. Having very little as a child growing up in the post-Depression years left an impression on me that it was smart to find another use for something that was about to be discarded. I have managed to collect quite a few things over the years that will be useful for something someday. I cannot be responsible for that day not showing up on time. I can still see the look of disdain on my youngest son's face when he discovered my stash of old radio vacuum tubes. I finally gave in and threw them away so he could sleep at night. Hope I do not see them for sale on the Web one of these days.

As a child, I did not own a record player, so I used an old radio to build my first unit. Somebody told me it was possible to tune a radio to a blank channel and use the amplifier in the radio to connect the pickup arm on the needle to the volume-control switch. This I did, but with terrible results. A big chunk of hot, flaming metal wire came flying out of the radio and spun around the living room, glowing in the dark. I blew the lighting for the whole building. Mom was not impressed and was relieved when I enrolled in electricity class at school. However, things did not go much better at school.

We had a simple training schedule that involved drawing junction boxes showing the connections necessary to install a single light with a switch. If the drawing connections were correct, the teacher would then allow you to wire the job on the table and, after inspection, give you permission to plug it in. I worked very hard all year long and escalated my way up to the big job. I had to draw a parallel circuit involving twelve lights with four remote switches. I got through the drawing requirements and proceeded to go ahead with the construction.

This job was so large that it took up all the space on the thirty-foot table. I grew apprehensive as inspection time arrived. The teacher was well-qualified, having written some of the training manuals that were used during World War II to get the men up and running as fast as possible. Still, I thought it a little strange for him to wear one shoe that was brown and the other black during class. He caught me passing a note to some of the other kids in the class and made me bring it to him. The note read, "Check out the teacher's shoes." After composing himself, he explained that he usually went home at lunchtime and took a nap on a cot, under which he had stored a couple of pairs of mixed-colored shoes. He proceeded then to take a cursory look at the job and gave me the go-ahead to plug it in. I became an instant hero in high school, not because I had successfully taken on the toughest job in the book, but because of the fire drill called after I plugged it in. A blue streak of lightning went from one end of the table to the other, popping bulbs and wires and filling the room with black smoke from the burning wires. I had managed to clear the room in an instant as everyone ran for cover.

The teacher claimed that I changed a connection after inspection, but I had not. Must have been one of my friends. It was a funny sight to see the whole school streaming out of the building for a well-deserved afternoon break. I even noticed a hint of a smile on the teachers' faces.

12

Up until this part of my story, things sort of fall into order and follow a natural course of events. Therefore, what were the gods thinking when you consider the following chain of events? Am I supposed to believe in fate, or are the gods just having fun with names? Growing up in Jersey City, I was given the name of Jackie. To this day, my family members still refer to me this way. I have never been able to shake it. Is this important or just strange? You be the judge after digesting the continuing story.

As my military career continued, I moved to Otis AFB in Massachusetts. Getting to Otis was a freak accident. When you attend technical-school training after basic training, you receive a choice of assignments based on where you finish in the class grading. I had picked Fort Dix in New Jersey as one of the available assignments so I could be near home. Unfortunately, a person with a higher score got the assignment. I then decided that I might as well take a base far away. I picked Lowry in Denver and had it for about three minutes when one of my other classmates begged me to switch with him because his folks lived about a mile away from the base. He had drawn Dow AFB in Maine. I agreed to make the switch because it was on the East Coast. Another person from the class approached me on giving him a shot at Dow because of family ties, and I wound up taking Otis AFB all in the space of five minutes. I hope their lives were OK because of fooling with fate. One of the ironies of my life is a transfer offered to me by a company many years later, which put me back in Denver, one mile away from Lowry. My children are forever grateful for the chance and opportunity to grow up in Denver. I took the kids for a trip back to my hometown and gave them a ride over to Manhattan on the subway. Frankly, they were very happy to arrive back in Denver. It was almost like visiting a very different world for the kids, a world they did not understand, and that made them feel out of place.

The assignment I received to Otis AFB was more like getting a job in a new company. Gone was the strict military training. Now I was in the real air force sans the instructors. KP duty was alive and well, and I continued to participate on a regular basis. GI night was on Wednesday for cleaning the barracks, but for the most part, it was like having a regular eight-to-five civilian job.

After settling in at Otis, the first sergeant called an all-hands meeting and asked if anyone had any carpet-laying experience. I told him, "If he could find a good Hungarian, I would be a good helper." He laughed, but we could not find one. A week later, the story leaked that the thirty-fifth president of the United States might be spending some time at the VIP quarters and that it needed new carpet. The first sergeant recruited me to help with the carpet installation since I was the best choice he had. We proceeded to get the job done, and then I took the liberty of sitting in "the rocking chair," which had become a symbol during the president's years in office. I guess the White House kept a few extra chairs around in case the president had to visit different locations.

A friend who worked at the 551st Base hospital medical facility approached me earlier in the year to volunteer as a standby blood donor for emergencies that happen at the hospital on occasion. I agreed to his request and filed it in the back of my mind. Six months later on the way to the mess hall, the blood call came in. Two other airmen were also on this standby list, but both were off duty and could not be located at the time of the call.

The president's wife admitted to the hospital for early childbirth required blood, so I donated two pints of blood to his First Lady (Jackie). This was not something special, except for the mistake of having it get out to the news media. Donating blood is a routine procedure, so I did not understand the fuss generated by the incident. I received a call from the front office after it happened and told that one of the reporters wanted to talk with me. I made the mistake of answering his questions and, in so doing, wound up giving him an exclusive story. This is totally in violation of base policy in that the base information officer should have handled the news release. As a way of saving face for the military, I had to visit the press conference. Sixty microphones and countless TV cameras greeted me, with reporters asking just about every question you can imagine. The message spread all over the world and caused a lot of embarrassment for all concerned. I retreated to my barracks and tried to hide after the hospital commander chastised me for trying to run the hospital while he was supposed to be in charge. That did not seem exactly fair at the time because I actually saved him a lot of bad press by refusing the doctor's offer to stay overnight at the hospital for observation. I kept visualizing the headline YOUNG AIRMAN HOSPITALIZED AFTER HELPING DEMOCRATS and thought that it would not look good for the president. I think I set a world record by donating two pints of blood at the same time.

It left me a little drained, but the officer on duty ordered me a nice steak, and I felt great afterward. If nothing else, it was the most famous donation of all times. It is rare that a blood recipient knows the origin of the blood. Three days of a nonstop roller coaster ride that left me back where I started from, more confused than ever about life's meaning. How could a street urchin from Jersey City wind up interfacing with one of the most important women of our times? The gods were playing games again. In truth, I have to explain that the doctor gave me a glass of orange juice in between pints. I was a little light-headed afterward, but with no permanent damage.

It was routine to see the president flying in on his helicopter at Otis. Therefore, I made the connection in my mind that he might stop to say, "Thanks, mister," since my unit was right next to the VIP quarters. I do not know if you can imagine the fear associated with the possibility of the president stopping by to say thanks. It never happened, but that is what I lived through for a few days. In addition to being a concerned father, the president was busy that day negotiating a nuclear treaty and running the country, so I was not upset that we did not meet. Sadly, the First Lady lost her baby, and a chapter in history closed. The president died a few months later in Dallas at the hands of an assassin. It really hit home for many people stationed at Otis. I was reluctant to write or talk about this over the years since I don't want to capitalize on their family name, but it's a piece of my puzzle makeup that had a profound impact and altered my life. The First Lady has since passed on, and I feel that a piece of me went to the grave with her. Life sure takes some strange twists and turns.

Life at Otis was never the same after this incident, and I was happy to receive an overseas transfer shortly afterward. I finally made it to Fort Dix when my father unexpectedly passed away while I was out of the country. This came as a real shock in that Dad was the kind of person who never took an aspirin. The captain in charge told me to sit down because he had some bad news to tell me. I remember preparing myself for the news that something had happened to my mom because she had such a chronic health condition all her life. I was in no way prepared for it to be my father. I flew home on emergency leave to attend his funeral, and since I had such a short time left on my assignment, the military advised I would not be returning overseas. It was difficult to say goodbye to my friends and close another chapter of my life. I remember being bitter for a long time, that my father and I did not get a chance to say goodbye (much like the president's family). I also recall reflecting on the simplicity of my father's funeral compared with the pomp associated with the president's passing. It turned out that my father was more important to me, but there was no riderless horse or caissons at the event to commemorate his years spent in the trenches of life and the sacrifices he made raising a family.

After the funeral, the government reassigned me to the base closest to my home and wife for discharge. It seems they lost my records and could not discharge me until they located them. They were, of course, down the hall in someone's in-basket; but it took about four weeks to find them.

While mourning the loss of my father, I had the task of cleaning out the fifty-five-gallon drums behind the chow halls; after, I delivered the drums full of leftover food to the pig farms each day. One month after being discharged, I received a letter from the treasury department advising that they had overpaid me for one day of service and that I had to return the one day's wages before I experienced the full weight of the U.S. government's ability to collect outstanding debts. Thanks, mister.

13

I just started to realize that I am growing old. This was not a planned thing; it just happened one day all of a sudden. I got up to have breakfast and read the newspaper and found that I could not focus my eyes on the print. This was my first clue that things are changing and that I am no longer in boot camp. One of the observations I have made since this scary day is that older people are carrying many problems on their backs. Younger people have a tendency to look away when they see older people, with their bowed backs and that faraway look in their eyes, walking in the shopping malls. They have already done most of the things you have not even thought about doing and have the scars to prove it.

Not only is their skin all wrinkled; their minds are in the same kind of shape, tired and confused. They worry about how they are going to pay for all the sins they have committed but got away with temporarily. It is similar to the situation where the rent is due, but you have no idea about where the money is going to come from.

Inside that body is the same spirit that you woke up with this morning, another new day of fun and games. The elderly have fewer of them left and want to have fun but, by now, realize that they are like an old car, prone to breakdown and an eyesore in certain locations and situations. Deviation is the tool they use to escape the inevitable audit of their lives that will occur in the near future.

I went to the grocery store recently and met an elderly woman by the banana display. I simply asked, "Getting your potassium for the day?" and got myself into a very interesting ten-minute conversation. The storyline centered on the days she spent as a cheerleader before she got all wrinkly and needed a little energy boost. She ended the chat by thanking me for taking the time to talk with her, adding that most people never stop to chat with strangers.

The gaming casinos are a great and popular pastime for seniors. They do not go to win because they now realized that money could not buy happiness. Rather, it is one of the few places that they can go and feel comfortable fitting in with the other players. If you are having a party, it is normal behavior to select your guests for compatibility. Age is one of the items you consider before mixing your guests, and the older set has a tendency to be out of the parties. I have met more true friends at the casinos who feel comfortable talking and sharing their thoughts and assets than I have met in my entire lifetime. Can you imagine asking your neighbor at a slot machine next to you to loan you some money and having them say yes? It happened to me. Talk about truly sharing people! At best, the casinos are social meeting places much like the neighborhood churches—highly promoted, costly, and serve as a place of belonging, validating that you are one of the lonely lost souls in the crowd. Both places compete for the almighty dollar.

It is somewhat dumb on the part of the casino owners who fail to make the atmosphere user-friendly for the seniors. Music from the '40s and '50s would go a long way in making the crowd stay longer in a happy environment. The younger crowd does not have the same discretionary spending power as the seniors; they should be busy working and raising their families instead of gambling!

I did a stint of one and a half years as a casino marketing manager and talked with many lonely seniors. As a rule, it was difficult to get them to sign up for a player's club card for fear they would be identified as one who had violated their church-circle group. In addition, if their kids found out that they were playing, they would lose their checkbooks and invite a quicker trip to the nursing home. It is wild and sinful to participate, so it is wise to do it quietly. In any event, I found out where my money went—some to the casinos, but a great deal more to education and doctors.

Did you know that some doctors have four different price schedules that they do not show you before treatment? Instead, they use them to fit the occasion. The poor pay on the installment plan. If your medical insurance is from a major company, they charge the standard fee. If you walk in for treatment after having an accident, you can expect hospitalization for tests to rule out a bunch of conditions. Each day that you are there, expect to see the doctor come in and read your chart and bill your accident policy $100 or more for making the five-minute stop, sometimes before you are given a pill and then again later to check on the results of the medication. If he is lucky enough to have six patients in the hospital on the same day, he is earning $600 for thirty minutes of work. If you are on Medicare, expect to have every conceivable test in the book because the government has deep pockets.

Have you ever seen a doctor driving an old car to work? It will never happen in our lifetime! We have a tendency to treat our doctors to whatever they want to take. We even give them special parking spaces in each of the hospitals so they can collect their money faster.

However, wait—what goes around comes around. One of the biggest rip-offs in this area is allowing the doctors to ride herd on when you can renew your prescription. If you know that you have the same condition that you had last year and that the pills you took then will work just fine, why do you have to take time off from work to visit the doctor again? Are we just stupid, or can we be trusted to take care of ourselves? The body talks to you when you get an infection. It would be great to buy a bottle of penicillin over the counter when you need it! It is too bad that the doctors have them locked up under their control.

The latest fad is making an appointment and finding that your doctor is busy, and they have sent in a physician's assistant. Same price but first, you have to distribute your history again and educate the PA. I have never seen a doctor who reads your file the day before and makes a game plan for your office visit. The file is reviewed when you are in the office, and hopefully, the test results have arrived in your file in time for the visit. At best, your file receives a cursory look and not a lot of thought given to your real problem. I have noticed over time that doctors do not dispense sympathy. If you are going to the doctor for social reasons, save your money and take responsibility for your own health.

I guess it is wrong to condemn all the doctors. Some are good. I support a group of physicians in New York who travel the world doing free cleft lip surgery for poor children. The group is small in number, but I guess it takes all kinds of people to make up the world!

14

"Have you noticed that some of the people in heaven wear silk robes, and other folks are wearing just some kind of terry cloth robe?" asks Gautama. "The Creator has this new reward system based on what he finds in his interviews. He turns some of the mortals into angels and sends them back to earth for an extra life."

"He's sure a crafty guy," blurts Muhammad.

"Well, what do you expect?" asks Abraham. "He's the Creator. When he gets an idea, he just runs with it. Saying no to his whims or fighting him on his ideas is like saying no to a nine-hundred-pound gorilla. You never want to do that."

Abraham interjects, "I was over at the angel's dorm rooms the other day and was amazed at their digs. They have everything you could ever want or imagine. It is tough to qualify to be an angel, and the rewards have to make up for what they have to do to qualify. First and foremost, they have to feel the thorns while they are in their first life."

"You mean suffer?" asks Gautama.

"Big time. The more pain they go through, the better their chances of making the cut. You know, skipping the second life is a tough assignment. Few if any make it!"

I have mourned the passing of many of my friends; and I have had to sit by quietly, watching other friends suffer, with no defense to offer them as they fought the dreaded diseases in their lives. You want to rage against the injustice, but it doesn't help. Why would the gods want to pass such suffering on to a woman, who routinely helped blind people to cope, and never missed a Sunday Mass? She surpassed her tithing at her church with her ability to make terrific spaghetti gravy. I loved her as much as I loved her gravy. The example her husband gave to others around him of standing by and helping her cope was inspirational. My friends and I had an ongoing twenty-five-year contest about who made the best cheesecake. As my long-overdue gift, I am declaring that I came in second.

I recall receiving a frantic late-night phone call many years ago from my neighbor Ruth who said, "Come quick." Her husband, Bill, had hit the floor. Bill was in his early seventies and living on oxygen in poor health. I rushed over with my oldest son and found Bill cold and not breathing. We did our best to bring him back until the fire department arrived. He survived and went on to serve as the hand-holding husband. Months later, Ruth developed stomach cancer and died several weeks later in a hospice. It was the most miserable death I had ever witnessed. She suffered through a complete wasting down to the bone with unbearable pain.

My daughter tried to bring her some comfort through guitar music and soothing songs at the hospice, and she made me very proud. Bill never recovered from the loss of his wife and died six months later a lonely disillusioned man. It was just five years after the big shock of finding their only son was shot and killed at age thirty-five by a jealous suitor. Go figure, why him and not us?

For me, this was a lesson learned on how to approach the real meaning of life. We are born to ease the suffering that goes on around us, not to add any additional pain to the world. Life itself will supply all the pain unimaginable—much more pain than we are capable of handling. It is somewhat sad that I did not have exposure to the lesson earlier in my life. I didn't find out until I was in my fifties. It turns out to be the driving force for me to write it all down for the people who will follow.

I am writing this story near the fifty-fifth anniversary of the end of the Korean War. It makes me think about the approximately thirty-six thousand young American men and women and the three million people whose lives were cut short because of the predators who started the war in Korea. It helps to put things in perspective when you ask yourself, "Why was I spared, and what am I doing with this precious time and once almost-perfect body?" I want to say "Thanks, mister" to all whose names I didn't know but have given their lives and bodies in defense of their country so that others might live. Somehow, it seems too little too late. Even at this late date, we still cannot account for the 8,200 missing in action from the Korean War.

Think about the carnage and creative loss that resulted from not having those veterans working, producing, and raising families. Then multiply that times the loss of their children who were never born. There might have been another great Thomas Edison or Thomas Gray in the group. However, we will never know! It almost makes sense to stop fighting in the trenches and instead use precision-guided weapons to rid the world of known predators and religious leaders who use the scriptures for their own benefit.

Wars have been going on for centuries; and I would be remiss not to mention the carnage from the Vietnam War, World Wars I and II, and the Civil War. Living, breathing men and women will never again feel the sun on their faces because of the thoughts and actions of a few lunatics. The Holocaust consumed approximately six million people because of letting predators rule our lives.

I spent a lot of time reading and rereading Thomas Gray's "Elegy Written in a Country Churchyard," looking for some of the answers to life's puzzles. Every time a new problem popped up, I would reach for the poem, look to the sky, and reach the conclusion that the prophets are crazy. Christ, Muhammad, Gautama, Abraham, Guru Nanak, where the hell are you? It is almost like looking for a cop when you need one.

The prophets are sitting up there having fun playing games with my life. If they have nothing to do and time on their hands, anything is possible. *Noninterference* is a good catchword they use when bad things happen. "Look at the stupid way that guy is living his life," they would say and laugh at the outcome.

If no one is in charge and taking an active interest in what I do, then I can do whatever I want with my life. My mother would say, "Everything costs something. Nothing is free." I didn't fully appreciate the wisdom of that bit of parental guidance until after the bills arrived. It makes it easier *not* to criticize your neighbor when you realize that they are in charge of their lives just as you are in charge of yours. The secret appears to be that even though we may have gotten shortchanged here on earth, with bad looks or less-than-perfect bodies, the rewards are the same for all of us in the future. Your neighbor will pay for his/her strange ways, shortcomings, overzealous greed, lust, and coveting. He or she will have a bill attached for their sins, but not yours. You get to ante up for your own activities, and the prices are not cheap. If you extend the definition of *neighbor* to include those whom you work with on a daily basis, you can appreciate the reward system that the Creator has in place. His system covers all possible situations. Let your neighbors have all the freedom they want. There is a price tag on each item or course of action. Knowing this information, is it still necessary to debate Roe versus Wade or to picket sites that practice things that go against our beliefs? If you believe in choice, then everyone should be allowed to choose as long as everyone pays his or her own bill.

The tough part is that it is a measured life. You are going to die, just like the millions before you. Look at some of the old classic movies of the '30s and '40s and marvel at the fact that all the players are no longer with us. Some of them were neat people that you would like to keep around and talk to and further enjoy, but it's not in the cards or part of the big picture. What is death anyway? Is death just a journey that we are taking? Where, when, and how did it start? In addition, the bigger question should be why. Some of us live on to a ripe old age, and others never make it past their early lives. Both get shortchanged for some unknown reason.

I marvel at the scene each morning going to work. Thousands of people all getting on the road at 7:00 a.m. Most of them get in line, obey the traffic signals, and cope with the traffic jams in an orderly fashion. Some are not coping at all. It is amazing to see them changing lanes, rushing through red lights, and trying to get a jump on the other cars. They are more important than their neighbors are, I guess. I refer to them as crybabies. Lesson 2 in life should be never cross a solid white line to get ahead of someone. Always wait for a broken white line before changing lanes. Do not put your blinker light on until you have checked to see that there is a place for you. It is OK to use your brake! All our insurance rates would go down if we practiced the right-of-way rule.

15

Abraham looks over and notices Muhammad and Gautama in heavy conversation. "What's wrong? You look like you're into some heavy thinking."

"Oh, I just got back from a tour of that massive building that the Creator built," says Muhammad. "I was surprised to find that they have this huge data-processing facility over there, full of weird people who are not like you and me. They are very quiet people who do not communicate with you when you pass them in the hall. They never say hello for some reason."

Gautama adds, "Do you remember the discussion we had a few weeks ago? I mentioned the givers and the takers that exist in life. The takers are usually made up of political appointees who go to the front of the line at every opportunity and people who never consider the feelings or needs of others as they rush through life, changing lanes in traffic to gain an advantage. We have many greedy souls in the building. They are all there, but not comfortable. The people in heaven have tremendous needs, and there is a highly trained service staff made up of, you guessed it, the takers."

I stole an apple when I was a kid because I was hungry and thought I was justified in my actions since I thought of myself as inferior. This was the first time I realized that Roscoe had company inside my head. I named this other voice Sam for no good reason. These two individuals are always taking opposite positions on every subject. Roscoe takes a conservative position on pretty much all subjects while Sam is a complete lunatic. Sam has gotten me in more trouble over the years because of his favorite line of advice, "You'll never know if you don't try it." They don't fight with each other but instead force me to make all the decisions. Fortunately, a young adult stopped me and made me give the apple back to the fruit vendor. I think he was a friend of Roscoe. It never occurred to me that this vendor was working hard to make a living to support a family and that I could do the same. Thanks, mister. I can never take back the bad act, so over the years, I have dropped a few dollars into the charity buckets every time I think of how bad it was to steal.

That one simple indiscretion has cost me a small fortune just because I have a good memory. The lesson has stayed with me all my life and serves as a guide. When I think about shaving a little time off my employer's work or gaining an advantage of some kind at the expense of others, I remember that it is wrong. I never found out what his name was, but thanks again to someone who took the time to influence my future years. The point here is that the Good Samaritan did not have to stop me. He could have shrugged it off as though it was none of his business. Instead, he ran after me and gave me some free guidance that was very valuable to my future.

Couples start off together playing house and wake up thirty years later to find that their children have grown up, moving to a bigger and better house while their backs were turned for a second. That great secret is missing in the instruction manual. It goes by fast. Most of the time, we are so busy with our chores that we do not see the time passing. Birthdays are celebrated one at a time, and we do not feel any real change until later in life. After all your uncles and aunts have passed away, you start to realize that you have replaced them as the senior members of the family, and then it begins to sink in.

I received a letter saying that the high school I attended was having a forty-year reunion. I thought, *This must be a mistake, and they sent it to me in error.* I didn't recognize many of the names, but the memories were still fresh in my mind. It seems like it was just yesterday when the cherry bomb (a big red firecracker) went off in the auditorium in grade school. The classes were changing at the time, and everyone used the auditorium as a crossing zone to get to their next class. The explosion was loud and followed by an authoritative voice, which said, "NOBODY MOVE!" As the smoke billowed from behind the radiator, all those in close proximity still felt the urge to run. Of course, they all became immediate bombing suspects. It seems the teachers had never heard about delayed fuses on cherry bombs. Even us dumb eighth graders knew enough to set a delayed fuse so you can give yourself time to take cover from the shrapnel. The case was never solved and closed after graduation.

Memory is a funny animal in that certain things are stuck in your head that defy time. My earliest recollection related to pain was experienced in kindergarten. I was sitting on my desk chair, and all of a sudden, a part of my body started to grow. I had to check it out; so I opened up my pants to investigate, discovered that the part, which I had not considered special, had gotten very hard and was hurting. When the teacher asked me what was wrong, I showed her that my thing was very hard. I remember her telling me that it would go away and not to worry. She then pinned me with a special note that

I was instructed to give to my mom. That was the first time that I remember hearing the phrase *Sweet Jesus* and the first time I saw my father smile ear to ear. I get a chuckle remembering the incident, and I like to contribute.

It helps to regress so you can understand the purple hair and pierced ears and tongues on the hard bodies you bump into on the way to the mailbox. They are going through their lives just as I did, lost and alone, seeking answers.

I still don't like the *boom boom* sound coming from the cars pulling into the apartment complex. I can't imagine someone being in the car while that is going on. I decided to give them the benefit of my doubt and tested it out myself to see if I was missing something. I got a copy of "Swanee" by Al Jolson on a new CD, turned the volume up all the way on the car stereo, and parked in front of the shopping center. *You crazy teenage bastard*, I thought to myself. I had found the secret to time travel. Therefore, I put it all in perspective and moved on.

16

"The second thing I have on my agenda today relates to my new plan to have a two-stage judgment process for the new millennium. Instead of casting people down to hell for their sins, I am going to give them a second life as the animals that they behaved like in their first life. It will give them a little more time to adapt to the future pain that they have coming their way or serve as a penance for those who are not truly qualified to be in my kingdom but who show some promise. I had a conversation with Noah last night, and he contributed some tips on animal control, which I found interesting. Noah still hasn't gotten over the ark trip and complained about the terrible odor he had to live with, having all the animals cooped up in such tight quarters." The Creator pauses for a moment and adds, *"It got me thinking that maybe a better way to handle my judging-man duties would be to just automatically transform the mortals when they die on earth into the animals they will become in their second life. That way, they will not have to visit the pearly gates and leave unwanted deposits. There is no sense in getting our streets of gold all mucked up with droppings. Boy, all it takes is one surprised sinner who thought he was on a free ride to make things really unpleasant. After the mortals do their penance as animals, I can have them up for their final interview."*

You have heard the expression "May God strike me dead if I am lying." So I am sitting here worrying what will happen to me for revealing these precious secrets of life and angering the Almighty by speaking in a blasphemous tone. I looked up the word *blaspheme* in the dictionary, and it seems to be a Greek word. It is definitely not one of God's words, but I think the religious institutions have gotten a lot of mileage out of it over the years. Anytime their authority to run our lives is threatened in any way, they use it to condemn. "It's all about cash flow." Maybe I will make it to somebody's hit list for speaking out. Perhaps I should let you go off and make the same mistakes that I made. However, I love my family and neighbors! Still, if you watch the nightly weather reports, thousands of bolts of lightning hit the earth each day. If someone is really aiming at me from the heavens, you run the risk of never getting to the end of this story. Maybe I am on a special mission from a higher authority, and I do not have a clue.

Somewhat gutsy for an old person to think these thoughts, but I am toying with the idea of starting a completely new religion to save the world. You could say, I had a revelation. Most people believe in revelations.

Have you noticed that most of the world's problems center on the radical beliefs of our religious leaders who saw it fit to write down and pass on to us the "rules." Do not eat meat on Fridays, you must not live in peace with your neighbors because they are infidels, etc. The leaders are dead; let them rest in turmoil for all the problems they left behind. The whole world is trying to cope with approximately six books written centuries ago without the aid of a spell-checker, and each one contradicts the other. Maybe it would be a good six-month experiment to pack away our Bibles or our quick reference books to the Qur'an, Vedas, Adi Granth, and Torah because they seem to be adding stress to our lives. Likewise, looking for more Dead Sea Scrolls can only add more confusion. We are in enough trouble already, and they will not help either. I am about to disturb some people and add a lot of pain to my own life but all for your benefit. If one of the religious leaders or the scriptures you have put your faith into promises eternal life, be careful. You might live on as a scorpion, taking up residence on the hot desert floor with all the other bad guys. The gods live dull lives and look for all kinds of kinky ways to beat the boredom. Here is a way to beat the system. Try my new religion. The church doctrine will be based on the principle that you will be reincarnated and come back as an animal, reminiscent of the kind of animal you were when in your human form.

It must be evident by now that I am not a rocket scientist or a scholar because I knew nothing about reincarnation until I looked it up in the dictionary. I came across words like *metempsychosis*, *karma*, and *kabala* and quickly lost interest. The fairy tales we all grew up with have many incidents of frogs being turned into princes and all sorts of magical stuff that we cast aside as not believable, so it must be make-believe. However, it started me thinking—trust me, I am not talking about magic, but some of the scariest events you can imagine. Can you envision what it would be like encased in an animal's body, with all the memories of past sins to carry with you, during your second life? With no voice to speak the words "I'm sorry" or pockets in which to carry around your cash? I cannot speak for the kangaroos that have those little built-in pouches because I think it would be a life-altering event to reach in and check them out. However, your days of running to the store to buy food or special toys are over. Spend it if you have it because it is not going with you on your journey. These are my original thoughts based on experience and not on research. I am sure that there must be some scholarly dissertation on reincarnation founded in the scriptures, but I have not read them.

Have you noticed the characteristics of the animals you see in your daily life? We have man's best friend, the dog, who would do anything for you as long as you feed him. Most of the people you consider your neighbors and friends will be reincarnated in this class. Pretty good folk who only have minor screwups for which to repent. The Creator snaps his fingers, and surprise, you die and then wake up in a small cage with people gawking at you in a pet-store window. More than likely, you will have litter buddies that will be just as confused and scared over the transformation from human form to that of an animal to keep you company. On the surface, this does not seem like such a bad deal. Your owner will feed you daily. But consider for a moment that the lawyers have created a fear frenzy in the suburbs, advising people to have all their animals neutered in case they jump the fence and jazz a neighbor's pet. What a downer to have no sex in the second life and no voice to complain. Cats will also be a large category of people going the route of a second life. This could get a little rough in that cats are supposed to go through nine near-death experiences before continuing on their journey through the universe. This might be your reward for some of the hurt and pain you caused as a human. Another thing to think about is, what human family will you be assigned to, and where do they live? We currently have about seventy million dogs and eighty million cats in the United States, all needing a home.

Around my old home, pussycats were known as alley cats, and they sang a lot. It was easy for me to turn out as a dog person instead of a cat person because the memories of dead cats in the neighborhood were very vivid and negative. Cats were always getting hit by cars and roasting in the sun, with flies all over them, for days on end. Nobody would bother to clean up after the accidents and give them a proper burial, except one of the local veterans in the neighborhood.

He came home from World War II, a little strange and shell-shocked. I guess he got used to seeing wholesale carnage, and it did not bother him. He was a sharing person who would pass out bullets and other souvenirs from the war to the local kids. He gave me a bronze star to play with, which I did not have any knowledge of at the time. He earned it for valor in combat on the front lines.

I don't know if you have given it much thought, but most animals do not have hands to use for eating. On many nights, it was common to hear a chorus of cats moaning away the night because they were hungry. Buckets of water would fly out the tenement windows in an effort to get some relief from the soul-wrenching sounds.

Squirrels, chipmunks, and koala bears have things a little better and can fend a little for themselves with their small hands. Life for an animal can be tough. Picture the fox and her nightly chore of finding some food for herself and her litter. In her lonely life, she will probably find a weaker animal to kill and eat—uncooked, of course! Suddenly, the expression "She's a foxy lady" takes on a completely new meaning.

Here's a scary thought—prairie dogs are probably the most persecuted little creatures we have living in our neighborhoods. They have hands for eating but don't pursue other animals for food. They live off the land and protect one another from predators by posting lookouts when they come out of their little underground homes. However, man, in his infinite wisdom, tries to gas or poison them at every opportunity. It might be good to pause and observe the lessons they teach on getting along with their neighbors. I drop a handful of peanuts when I walk by, just in case I am right about the second-life puzzle piece.

So how did I arrive at this crazy notion? Did I have some kind of religious experience? you ask. Well, that incident in Texas with the rattler left me a little goosey about snakes. I was so goosey at the time that I damned near caused a small riot at a local restaurant that was serving rattlesnake cocktails.

I had just hired a campus coordinator for an assignment at an out-of-state college and was taking him to dinner at a fancy restaurant to celebrate. Little did he know what lay ahead of him. Looking at the rattlesnake cocktail listed on the restaurant menu caused everyone to remember and tell his or her personal snake story collected over the years. The air became thick with unpleasant stories. I cannot recall any that was worse than mine, but I really felt uncomfortable because of the conversation.

The waiter at the restaurant came out and asked if anyone would like to visit the kitchen and witness the chef preparing the snake cocktails. I declined, but my guest and a few of the people at the adjoining tables thought it would be educational. Before they left, I gave them explicit instructions not to bring back any rattles for souvenirs or fun and games. I envisioned how I would feel watching the cook prepare the entrée and felt no good could come of it. Sitting with my back to the kitchen, I expected the worst. I thought, *Some jerk is going to sneak up behind me with a tail rattle, and I'm going to have a heart attack.* As it turned out, I was right in a way. They all came back, looking a little green as the snakes were still thawing out and slithering all over the cutting table. Everyone returned to his or her seat, and I thought, *Great, I get to live another day.*

However, as I turned to comment to one of the couples at the next table, the waiter, ever so quietly, came up next to me and brushed against my suit lapel as he was putting my dinner plate in front of me. I knew I had ordered a steak, but all I could see was a plate full of snakes. The imagination of the mind is unfathomable. My reaction was instantaneous. My chair flew back twelve feet on the speedy rollers, and I let out a whoop as I jumped up. Six people at the other tables were into the act also because they thought the snakes were loose in the dining area. They jumped up at the same time and joined me with screams while the waiter was trying to juggle the six plates on his arms, panicked, yelling, "What did I do? What did I do?"

This is no lie; it took five minutes to stop laughing after the incident. Each time the waiter came back, he made sure to announce his visit by saying, "I'm coming by again." This only added to the fun for the evening. I'm sure my guest had a few reservations about me and what he had gotten himself into, but he kept his thoughts to himself.

I was determined after that to face my fear and tried to overcome the problem by visiting the herpetology display at a local zoo. Let me tell you, the zoo I visited had one hell of a large anaconda in a big glass cage, which caught my eye and personal attention right off the get-go. This snake was a good eight inches around and at least eighteen feet long.

The main room was dimly lit to avoid the snakes having a clear view of you as you stand in front of their glass cages. This cuts down on the number of times they bump their noses on the glass when they try to strike out at your movement. The lighting also creates a somewhat spooky feeling to the room and causes the little hairs on the back of your neck to get somewhat excited. The anaconda's cage, showcased right in the center of the room, stood out and drew your attention. When I walked in, I thought he was dead or just a stuffed model; but as I got closer to the glass, it turned out that he was just sleeping. I stood there thinking to myself, *Boy, you must have done something really bad, like nailed somebody to a cross, to merit the life confinement of sitting on a large tree in a glass cage, having to eat large live rats for dinner.*

With my thoughts permeating through the glass in a telepathic way, he opened one eye as if to say, "You have found the secret." The one open eye was enough to send chills through me as though I had opened a coffin to look at the remains of a decaying body in an ancient crypt. For a moment, I felt the fear that I imagined a rat must feel being stuck in a corner of the cage just before suppertime. A feeling of being in the ancient past came over me. It was as though I was witnessing the Crucifixion. I felt I was in the presence of pure evil. When the snake opened his other eye, it felt like I was looking into his soul. The soul of a killer given a sentence from which there was no relief. It signaled to me that it was time to move on.

Unfortunately, I have another problem; I have this thing about heights and tall buildings. You know that tingling feeling you get in your legs when you get too close to the edge of a balcony? My legs feel like someone is pouring concrete down my pant legs when I even think about the edge of a building. I believe it is a leftover condition from my earlier years. This was the same feeling I had while standing in front of the cage.

I know now that it was wrong for me to freeze in that spot. King Pilot (I think that was the snake's name) had other thoughts and decided to kill me for disturbing his world by recognizing his sins and true identity. He took a flying leap off the tree and tried to consume my head. You haven't died until you have seen the inside of an anaconda's mouth at eye level. His tonsils went on forever down the sides of his wide-open mouth. This attack was not just a wild animal's instinct to eat, *it was personal.*

It was *quite a revelation.* Thankfully, the glass was thick and did not shatter, but I will bet he had a pretty sore mouth from the force of the blow on the glass. I had already conceived a plan in my mind in case the glass did break. I was going to drop dead on the spot. I relive the incident every time I see someone wearing thick-lens glasses.

I was watching a movie recently and was surprised when a young man with thick round glasses was talking telepathically to a big snake, thirty-eight years after I visited the zoo. I have spoken of my story many times over the years, so it is possible that someone picked up on the incident.

I tried to leave my chair when the snake got loose on the movie screen, but the concrete in my legs stopped me. It's funny how some minds travel on the same pathways. I'm thinking of not forgiving my son who hawked the movie by telling me I had to see it but forgot to warn me about the snake part.

I think my two boys have a get-even streak in them for all that I put them through in their early years. Years earlier, my eldest son left a colorful, lifelike rattler right under the garbage-pail lid for me to find when it was my turn to do the nightly chore. Nice guy! Fortunately, I noticed the tail sticking out; and it was not moving, so I got through it realizing that boys will play!

Getting back to my new religion thing, I have to ask you the question, Were you a pussycat, a lovable teddy bear, a dog, a snake in the grass, or a large rat in your lifetime? How are you living your short life? Can you answer the question regarding your next identity? Will you be one of the prairie dogs eating my peanuts? Will you turn out as a deer or antelope in the gun sights of a hunter? Will you return as a cow or lamb being led to the slaughterhouse? Maybe you were just gullible and placed your faith in some crazy religious leader instead of listening to your heart?

Think about it, and consider changing before it is too late. As long as you are still breathing, you have an opportunity to right a wrong. You can't do anything about it after you are dead. Don't believe in the old saying that it doesn't matter how many people you hurt or kill because they can only hang you once. You will be forgetting how long a period of time you will get to sit in the zoo cage and eat rats for supper. Contemplate the power of Almighty God. If he was able to create the universe in seven days as outlined in the book that you believe in, imagine what he could do to you in the blink of an eye!

Do you remember the serpent that talked to Eve in the Garden of Eden? I do. I know all the snakes in my neighborhood by name. I bet you talk to your pet or try to communicate in some way. I bet you think of them as almost human with feelings and that they are part of your family. Pet owners spend millions of dollars each year trying to make their animals as comfortable as possible but fail to consider their human neighbors. For fun, try using mental telepathy, and see if you can find out whom they were in their last life. It would be great if you could get back to their families to let them know that they are OK. If you want to try an experiment, imagine what animal all your friends and neighbors will come back as in their next go-around. I will bet you would not want to turn your back on some of them. The next time you reach for your pet cleanup tools, think about your neighbor and ask yourself if you would give them as much consideration as your pet.

Each of us will come back as something. However, there is no difference between a rich rat and a poor one, an educated one versus an ignorant one. We will all come back to grace the dinner plate of some other animal, and I bet they all taste terrible. Your original DNA plays a big part in determining your second-life assignment. It's not fair in a way, but if your grandfather was an SOB and you sat at his knee to learn, you might be in trouble. He probably came back as a big lion, and depending upon the improvements you made in your life, you could come back as a kitty cat. You will belong to the same species but will have a much better second life. Remember, you can't talk your way out of it because you cannot speak!

Have you ever thought about the fact that all the animals look the same? They don't have any facial characteristics to define their identity. One tiger looks the same as the next tiger. They all kill if you get too close. God, they are almost human!

Who knows, I might be right about the revelation, and nobody believes me. Please, go ahead and check it out at the local zoo. I'm a believer at this point, and there is no reason in the world for me to go back.

I haven't opened a church yet or collected any of that free money that people throw at their religious leaders or put in the collection basket to support their church through tithing. Nobody told me it was that easy! What a fool! If I could get organized and get a bunch of people to come hear me spout about my theory at a dollar a head, I wouldn't have to work another day in my life. I could hold special Saturday gatherings for those who like to sleep in on Sundays and then have two or three Sunday sessions for the truly dedicated who like to dress up for the occasion.

Well, how lucrative could this be? I really don't know, but I look at the Vatican, and I know that they started out small. There must be something to this as one church group leases an apartment in our complex and brings in two or three new divinity-student recruits to sell religious material in the area. I have to pay my rent each month, but this church group gets to write off the cost of the apartment as a business expense. The system looks a little strange to me.

17

Abraham greets Muhammad and says, "Some people are going to be really upset to find that they have to work in the third life. To supplement the service staff, the Creator has this Blue Card Program that allows special people to enter his kingdom on a work pass."

"Really?" asks Muhammad.

"Yeah, really," continues Abraham. "To qualify you have to have been a person who let others do their work for them or one who took advantage of the system. The free coupon flyers that got extra benefits for using the Corporate Travel Program make up a good part of the group."

"Not only that," Abraham adds, "since there is no sickness in our kingdom, this creates a real problem for the medical community. The Creator developed and announced a new program wherein a special gold dispensation seal is available on the Blue Card to the doctors, clergy, college professors, and CEOs who want in but who fail to pass muster under the normal rules. Since they have intelligence, they are trainable and are used to supplement the data-processing team."

"No kidding?" asks Muhammad.

Abraham continues, "While I was in the building, the chief IT manager (a former doctor) came rushing into the Creator's meeting and caused a big stir. He had a somewhat pained expression on his face and began to spill his guts. He told the Creator, 'Sir I don't know how to tell you this, but all the snakes in Ireland have disappeared. And in addition, something happened to the soil, and the people are starving because the potatoes won't grow.'

"The Creator laughed and said, 'Don't let this information leave your department. Let us keep it concealed. Have you not heard that the Lord moves in mysterious ways? I am trying to promote a religious myth and, at the same time, trying to teach the mortals about sharing. It has nothing to do with your computer system. The names of the snakes are still the same. You'll just have to change their addresses and show them as living in the ocean for a while.'"

Of course, if this new church thing becomes a reality, I will have to bring my wife along for company. Diamonds are cheap in comparison to hiring a full-time housekeeper. I bought one forty-three years ago and gave it to a pretty little thing for safekeeping. Since then, she has washed approximately 15,333 pairs of socks for me and put up with my ramblings about the bureaucracy of life, which turned out to be a worse assignment than the first one. This is all somewhat amazing in that our wedding almost did not happen, and it turned out very memorable.

I was still in the service at the time, so there were no fights over the wedding plans or the hundreds of other details that can break up couples before the final walk to the altar. My bride-to-be and I exchanged letters frequently, but there was about a five-day delay waiting for delivery. I had very little involvement in the planning of the ceremony. My wife decided to get married the day after Christmas, known as Boxing Day in other parts of the world. In England, the queen historically passed out boxed Maundy money sets on this day to the people who lived in certain sections of the city. The poor people who lived around her castle thought better of her as a result.

Three days before the wedding, I came down with an infection that required hospitalization. At the time, I was visiting the gym each day to get in shape and following up my exercise routine with a steam-room visit. I must have picked up a mold infection or something that knocked me on my ass. I explained to the doctor at the hospital that I had to be on a plane the next day. He said, "No way unless you can keep your temperature down for twenty-four hours." So I cheated a little and kept the thermometer between my teeth. I had a perfect excuse for not showing up for the wedding, and I blew it. I fooled the doctor (well, sort of); I boarded the plane and tried to make it home.

My glands blew up to three or four times their normal size on the flight, and I was concerned that the authorities would have me quarantined at customs when I arrived. I had to fly into Kennedy International and then take three buses to complete the trip. I tried to sleep and rest as much as possible, but it didn't help. Visualize a wet, limp tea bag, and you will have a good picture of what I looked and felt like two days before the big event.

I got into bed when I arrived at my parents' apartment and called the doctor to visit my bedside. In the old days, we had real doctors who visited the sick. When he found out that I was a ward of the U.S. government, he said that he could not legally treat me. The best he could do was to turn me over to the doctors at Fort Dix Military Hospital sixty miles away for treatment. I still needed a tuxedo and a bachelor party to make it a legal wedding, and he wanted to send me to another hospital. It just wasn't in the cards!

At this point, my future mother-in-law was getting a little concerned, and my wife-to-be was in a zone like you get in when you call bingo but haven't got the money in your hands quite yet. I called on all my pharmacy experience and told the doctor to open his little black bag and give me the broadest spectrum antibiotic he had. I think he realized the pain my mother-in-law would inflict on him if he didn't comply.

I don't remember the name of the medicine, but it worked. I called and ordered a tuxedo over the phone and got what I asked for. I must have been under the influence of the fever or something because it didn't fit when I got dressed for the big day. I missed the bachelor party, and my knees were knocking when I first spotted this beautiful lady walking down the aisle. I don't think it was the fever but instead, real fear. We made our vows and have kept them to each other over time. I kept thinking about running out of the church but luckily managed to get over the panic attack and concluded the ceremony.

This was just the beginning of our faithful day. Of course, it rained like hell; and our wedding pictures have plenty of umbrellas in clear view, along with my extralong tuxedo jacket sleeves. Later, we arrived at the wedding reception and found a really upset mother-in-law trying to deal with a small problem. It seems the caterer heard seventy-five guests instead of 175, and she was starting to go into shock. We were all shuttled into the bar while they tried to set up additional tables and place settings and find enough food to feed the masses. It took an extra hour and a half for the caterer to recover, but they comped the extra booze, so it wasn't too bad. I needed a good stiff drink now but was unable to have any due to my white-faced condition. Instead, someone mercifully gave Mom a real stiff Manhattan cocktail after a server accidentally tripped and dropped a large pot of food right at her feet. This was part of the recovery effort to provide more food, and it looked like we were going backward for a while. The food odors from the kitchen kept our hopes alive, and the guests finally ate dinner. Whew!

Despite the problems, everyone seemed to have had a good time at the reception. The extra booze before dinner helped the guests a lot. It was a little awkward trying to get through the day with all the upheaval, but it worked out OK. I had a little sip of the bubbly at the reception when no one was looking, and I think that was what cured me. The next morning, I awoke at the hotel to the sound of my mother-in-law's voice on the phone and immediately, I thought, *I'm in trouble for what I did with her daughter, and it's only been one night.* It turned out to be a false alarm; it seems the plane we were supposed to catch at 9:00 a.m. in Newark cancelled due to heavy rain at the airport, and we had to take a limo ride over to LaGuardia Airport to recover. The airlines had tried to reach us and could not, so Mom had to pass the message on to us.

To anyone contemplating married life, I can only say it's a roller-coaster ride, full of surprises, fun, and it's never smooth. Peaks and valleys come to mind when I consider the long ride. Some years are unbelievably bad with strange long honey-do lists and other years that defy grasping the definition of *happiness* because they are so great. Try as best you can to consider divorce only during the good years.

Early signs of impending trouble in my first year of marriage set the tone for the future. I should have heeded the warnings. My wife wished me forty years of bad luck for what I considered a minor indiscretion. How could someone get in trouble for shaving? It seems I was timing her labor pains during the birth of our first child, and since they were about fifteen minutes apart, I decided that would be ample time to get in a quick shave. Must have been a leftover lesson from boot camp. *Always shave before going out in public!* She has held this grudge for all these years.

I really worked hard on having a good marriage. For years, I practiced always putting the toilet seat down. This led to a 99.9 percent record that was instrumental in building a comfort zone for my pretty wife. She felt safe after thirty years of my flawless performance. The one time I screwed up just coincided with a late night trip that she took in the dark. Describing her screams that awakened me from a sound sleep is difficult. It is one of my finest memories. I had to help lift her out of the cold, wet toilet while she extolled my virtues in expletives I did not know she had in her vocabulary.

18

The Creator's assistants gather all the new angels together for a fireside chat. The lights blink, and the Creator arrives and announces that he is giving out a long overdue Angel of the Month award. "I can't think of a more worthy recipient than Fred, our own resident angel trainer. If you turn to page 178 in your Angel Training Manual, you will see an SOP (standard operating procedure) we adopted because of his quick thinking. This procedure documents an incident from many years ago, a young boy pushed from behind, sliding down this snow pile under a car that was passing in the street. It was not his time to go as I had other plans for him. Fred, being on duty that day, sprayed some rain and cold wind on the road and froze the street. This enabled the boy to slide down the street with the car instead of having to deal with the friction from contact with the asphalt on Dwight Street. As a result, I now have someone I can use as a messenger for the new millennium. Let's give Fred a big hand, and then I would like you all to say a special prayer for this boy because he has a lot more pain coming his way, and he is going to need some help! I picked on this kid because he speaks plainly without filtering his thoughts, and to some regard, he doesn't know when to shut up. He does not talk in parables like some people I know. His words are as clear as the sound of a bell. He hits you right between the eyes with the truth. He is somewhat different though. He never cries for something he wants. He seems to cry only when he sees misery. My friend Guru Nanak has tested him many times over the years with his dart bombs, and I have concluded that he is one of the people who can spread my word. He knows about Christ's crucifixion and what happened to him for spreading the truth, but it doesn't seem to bother him. It took a lifetime for me to show him some special things, and I am looking forward to real peace on earth when he helps to get the message out during the Age of Aquarius.

"I don't want you to get the wrong idea about this. He is not going to be part of the Second Coming. He's just a street urchin that I am giving a tough assignment because I think he can handle it, based on his past performance. I also want the puzzle scorekeeper to move some pieces around and slip his puzzle piece in between that tall handsome late-night TV guru and that dazzling daytime diva. Their names escape me, but you know whom I mean. I gave them their *success and high-paying jobs so they could share good things with their followers. It's nice that they are funny and entertaining at the same time. It will be a good test of their neighboring skills to see how they react to the street kid. I also think it would be a good idea to show him carrying a water jug in the puzzle picture so people will understand his assignment.*

The Creator was really busy when he designed us without making us look the same. We are all just a little bit different for a reason. It is up to us to find a solution for this puzzle.

I am disappointed that I am not handsome enough to appear on the cover of a magazine. This is a common thought shared by many. People stand in front of mirrors and don't like what they see staring back at them. "I am too fat or ugly" is an expression that many people use to excuse their lack of involvement in life. Hiding and blending in is a defense practiced by quite a few people. To fit into the big picture, it is necessary to have a unique identity unlike our neighbors. Never lose sight about how important you are to the completion of the puzzle. Consider the good looks of Mother Teresa (1910-1997) as a guide. You wouldn't want to call her a beauty, but consider how beautiful she will look in the big picture and what she was able to accomplish in her short time on earth. We each receive twenty-four hours each day to use as we see fit. Some men run a whole country with their time. Others take out the trash when the commercials come on the TV and then rush back to the boob tube. It is important to note that all sides of your puzzle piece touch the pieces next to you. We all have a responsibility to improve the big picture by fitting into our spot and feeling comfortable with our neighboring pieces.

I have figured out why people tend to stay in large cities instead of branching out and exploring the world. Fear—along with the thought that they can blend in with society, lose their personal identities, and not be held responsible for their own actions—is the motivating factor. When people do bad things, a certain amount of guilt builds up, and they try to hide behind closed doors. Some people lock themselves up for their entire lives and are afraid to say hello to their neighbors for fear of being exposed. Some people suffer trauma from the very strong Holy Scripture brainwashing they receive as children and forget that they are human. Each of us is capable of the worst imaginable sins, controlled only by situations over which we have little control. Peer pressure, curiosity, loneliness, lust, poverty, and the unknown are strong companions. We have all heard the theory that the people in New York City are a different breed of people. The expression *streetwise* is a way of explaining survival skills learned on the street. It is real, especially in our large cities. The average person from the Midwest would be like a fish out of water when visiting a large city and prone to having a lot of misfortune directed his way because of his trusting ways.

Something happens to people that causes them to be less trustful of their neighbors. The people in large cities are ripe for exploitation. All they need is a dictator to come by and promise better times, and a better life, by getting rid of the riffraff.

Can you imagine what life would be like if we had somebody like Hitler running our cities? For sure, the character of the people would change, and they would embrace it as a way of normal life. If you look at some of the old newsreels, you will see thousands of people cheering and encouraging Hitler to do his thing. After the discovery of the death camps, people realized they had made a big mistake. The people in the Middle East are going through this as we speak. The clergy tell people of the rewards of eternal life in heaven if they blow something up in God's name in a holy war. That has to sound pretty good to someone living in the hot desert in poverty with no hope of a comfortable life in the near future. It almost looks like a free ticket out—suicide with the blessings of the church. There are more people out there as bad as Hitler, and they need to be uncovered. If they are not improving people's lives, they have to go. I don't care where you take them; just get them out of the picture. Where are all our holy ones? Why the leaders do not stand up and make it right remains a mystery.

On the other hand, man is capable of the most imaginable good that can be spread around the world, controlled only by some of the same restrictive laws of man-made conditions in our minds. Peer pressure, lack of curiosity, loneliness causing depression, the feeling that revenge will improve our lives, and poverty brought about by nonwork are all strong conditions that we embrace.

19

Abraham and Muhammad knock on the Creator's living quarters door and ask to speak with the master. "Creator, the puzzle is getting all screwed up, and it's the fault of this new thing that the mortals invented called money. The puzzle pieces are killing their neighbors and stealing the money from one another. Things were much nicer when the mortals split their crops with one another."

"I know," says the Creator, "but do not go blaming the children. I had to invent money so we would have some way of judging the true ethical value of the recipients. It is educational watching how the mortals distribute it. Rest assured that I have it all recorded."

As they say good night to the Creator and walk into the night, Abraham whispers to Muhammad, "I had always heard that the Creator kept a special book that was used to record information on each of the mortals, covering all their good and bad deeds, but it seems he's gone digital. Now even the smallest details are in the record. I know you're laughing, thinking that the Creator doesn't have time for all that intricate accounting, but he played a trick on the mortals when he gave them a brain. What he really did was install a computer hard drive in their heads. When they show up for their final judgment, he downloads all their stored memories and thoughts and then adds the information to their records. I got a peek at some of the files, and you would be amazed at what some of these people are carrying around in their heads."

The unbelievably bad years I mentioned earlier relate to financial troubles caused by the tax system we live under, so I would like to digress and do a little bitching on your behalf, with the hope of lighting a small fire under someone who might be in a position of authority.

All our fearless government leaders advised us to start a savings plan at work, so we would have plenty of money to educate our kids when the time came to support the tenured class of educators. (Some have since died from eating high on the hog over the years.)

So you borrow the money to pay the tuition, which you can pay back to yourself with the interest going into your own account. Such a deal, sign me up! Then two years go by, and the pink slip layoff notice arrives. Your services are no longer required, but you must pay back your savings plan; or else the government will treat your tuition borrowing as a premature distribution, qualifying for a 10 percent penalty for trying to educate your kids. It almost seems like another type of religion exists based on greed (the tax code religion). At the time of this writing, the rules have changed again. You are now able to use the money for education without penalty. The tenured group of educators must have gotten to the leaders. Oddly, no one has called me to return my 10 percent. It just disappeared somewhere in Washington DC.

By the way, Congress is violating the rules by separating into two groups. Maybe that is why nothing gets accomplished. If I were king for a day, I would make them sit intermingled so they would talk to one another and maybe even make friends. I laugh when I see one group of party faithfully standing at the State of the Union address, and the other party sitting. It makes you wonder if any of the members in that group has a brain to use for serious thought.

I would like to see them address the issue of having all citizens treated the same. Before we give away any more foreign aid or build another killing machine, see if it is possible to exempt $1,000-per-month living expense for all renters before taxes.

Since my kids are all grown and educated, I worry they will miss some of the stress and things that I hold near and dear. They will grow up less prepared for the pressures of life and turn out as helpless yuppies. I do not wish it to happen, but can you imagine what would occur if the children of today had to face a major depression? I see the stories in the newspaper every day of people pulling the plug, taking their own lives, and stupidly taking the children along because they would not be able to cope without the breadwinner being around. Sure, their children's lives would be different, maybe even a little like mine. However, I will bet their lives encounter many rainbows along the way. Layoffs are not for sissies, so be prepared.

My solution for continuing my children's education, even though they are on their own, is to feign poverty. I call my kids and say the bank is after me to help them out with a large deposit, or my car payment is late, and they are coming to repossess. Any number of creative ideas will work to keep the children off balance and in the dark about their future inheritance. The one I like best is, "My rent is overdue," and they will have to come help me move my furniture into one of their houses. We have a standing rule at the house: never visit with Dad unless you bring your checkbook with you.

Both of my boys bought homes in the suburbs with resident snakes in their gardens, so I will not visit too often.

One of the problems with the work scene today is that all the kids we parents paid to educate are showing up with master's degrees and PhDs behind their names. To those I say remember the high school graduates (your parents) who paid the room and board and bills for college and protected the students from outside pressures. The people who paid the bills are the real workers of America. Most human resource departments run by college graduates whom we made the mistake of educating don't realize that they are handling gold when they see an older worker.

It is interesting to note that the man who holds a great number of patents (1,093 at last count), Thomas Edison (1847-1931), never finished grade school. He had a head full of ideas that did not originate in college. Just because you don't have a degree behind your name doesn't mean you should stop thinking great thoughts and following your dream. Only one in ten people ever bother to look for new ways of doing things. The rest are content going with the flow or the easy way.

Many of today's new graduates come to the job thinking that the proper way to set your priorities in life is God, family, and then the job. Some mix it up the other way by putting family first, God second, and then the job. If you are willing to sell your time to an employer, do not cheat by doing only half a job. The job will take care of your family by providing the money needed to pay the bills. You will get along better with your coworkers if you pull your own load instead of having them pick up after you. God help you if the job identifies you as a freeloader, and then the family goes hungry. Trust me, the gods do not care about your day-to-day problems.

I have been through four major layoffs in my working life, mainly because the tax code encourages corporate leaders to downsize and take the credits against profit and, in addition, because managers try to spend their budgets so they do not lose them. The idea of trying to find ways to do things cheaper and faster while keeping consumers employed fails to spark enthusiasm in the inner circles of most corporations. The end result is another visit to the human resources office trying to explain that "I didn't finish college because I was busy getting thirty-five years of on-the-job training in coping with the nine-to-five routine and paying for college electives to round out the education for my children." Finding the willpower to get up and attend work day after day is not easy, but after doing it for forty years, you would think that it would become a good record for judging a man's worth. I found that it was necessary to start over after each layoff due to the absence of a degree. Entry-level positions turned out to be the only solution.

It is difficult to reach the young graduates in the human resource office. I believe our schools make a big mistake in teaching our children competitive thoughts rather than sharing thoughts, which are more important. This makes them immune to the truth about life. Not "all men are created equal." Competitive sport brings home that point in a large way. If ten runners are in a race, they will finish first through tenth. We heap rewards on the winner but give no encouragement to the other nine runners, who will carry the loss with them as they interface with you in your daily work environment. We continue to seek out the person who can develop the best score on the balance beam while that person is passing through a brief phase of their lives. Why?

The same holds true for the academic side of life. People are graded all through their lives and made to feel that they are less than perfect and respond accordingly for the remainder of their working lives. Late in life, I discovered that I am a hearing learner as opposed to a visual learner. You cannot imagine how difficult that is for a child. I noticed that I had a tendency to rhyme words instead of visualizing them. Ask me to say the first thing that comes into my mind when I hear the words *sky*, *blue*, and *peach*; and I answer with rhyming things like *pie*, *true*, and *teach*. School was always conducted in a visual way and made it a difficult trip. I have always found it difficult to pay attention to the written page, but I also hear things better than most people and have the ability to visit a piano and play from the memory of the sounds. I guess what I am trying to say is, we all have special talents. I always came in last in the footraces, but I play the clarinet better than 75 percent of the world's population. That doesn't make me special, just a little different.

One of the things I learned along the way was that I made every mistake in the book trying to put food on the table and be a good parent. Books are available on how to avoid mistakes, but I could not hear them. It takes years to come out of the dark clouds and find your way.

I have been in the corporate world most of my working life, and I have noticed some people never find their way through the revolving door. The God-given talents they received at birth left them wanting in many areas. It has to be tough to grow up and find that you are limited in how much money you can earn for your family. They had the desire to work, but their skills and thinking powers inhibit their ability to get above the minimum wage for most of their working lives. The lessons I learned from these people are profound. Despite their problems, they still managed to project love for their fellow man and share their meager assets.

Starting in supervisory positions at a young age enabled me the opportunity to hire many of these less-than-perfect souls. I asked only for them to perform at their very best in an honest way and to share their problems. I am ending my career with the statement that I was never disappointed in their performance and never felt it necessary to fire one of the people that I hired. We talked a lot, and I counseled quite a bit; and usually, I was able to leave them with hope for the future. The current philosophy of hiring only the best qualified, highly educated people will lead to the destruction of the corporation. The underpinning, the real workers who hold up the buildings so the MBAs can fight for a bigger piece of the pie, are being driven out. Eventually, the MBAs will have to do all the work. The new incentive system of only rewarding the true movers and shakers in a company will come back to haunt some of the famous CEOs in this country (mostly, the CEOs who have retired with their excessive retirement packages earned on the backs of the lowest laid-off employee). I shouldn't bitch; the road ahead for these people looks pretty grim.

I am sitting here, trying to write a book about living to pass on all the good things I have learned to the masses that will follow. In effect, I am trying to say that my years spent on earth meant something. If a little frustration shows through, it's because life is filled with many frustrating situations. "I should have done this" or "I could have traveled in a different direction on that" seem to be statements reserved for the quiet time that arrives in the senior years. If children could realize their parents were little lost children when they were dragging them up, there would be no need for analysis. We tried to act like wise adults, but we made plenty of mistakes reacting to the pressures of life. For this we are sorry, but you can't take it back or change it. We have to carry our own baggage into eternity. As Mr. Shakespeare said, "The evil that men do lives after them, the good is often interned with their bones." We will continue to evolve as better humans if we don't repeat the sins of our fathers. Your kids will be better than you is one of life's lessons.

Roscoe and Sam continue to give me mixed signals in my head about how to live a good life as do the recorded religious sermons. As you mature, you have to filter through it and develop a plan that works for you.

Having lived and experienced life for quite a few years, I have developed a laundry list of definite no-nos that work for me. At the top of my list is never hurt another soul, either in a physical or mental way. It is wrong! Our lives should be spent trying to reduce pain not add to it. Carry this thought as you go off to work each day!

Secondly, never start an affair of the heart unless you intend to spend the rest of your life committed to bringing happiness to the other person. It's OK to test the waters by dating a lot of different people, but the smart thing to do is make a decision in between the dating. Trying to have multiple relationships all going on at the same time can be dangerous. When you have decided to share the seeds of your ancestors with someone special, it is time to make a commitment.

Third, never count yourself out of the game. We have all gone through some crazy years and come away ashamed of our actions and the bad things we have done in life. A little more of your shine disappears with each bad act. Simply replace each bad act with one good act during your remaining years. If you have already screwed up big time, make a bigger gesture to regain your self-esteem and move forward. If you have taken a wrong road, turn around, damn it, and go the other way. It is really that simple.

Fourth, never capitalize on the weakness or misfortune of others, especially when they are down. Recently, a neighbor evicted for failing to pay his rent at the apartment had his belongings placed at the curb in front of the building. At least ten misguided people stopped by and helped themselves to the remnants of his shattered life. When they wake up some day in a mouse hole, they will finally realize that it was the wrong way to treat a neighbor.

I think highly paid corporate executives fall into this same group. They are earning their million-dollar salaries, stock options, and golden parachutes at the expense of many laid-off workers. Stock options and extra benefits distributed to all workers on an equal basis would be a better solution. It is easy to say, "It's unfortunate that we had to have a reduction in force for business reasons," while hiding the fact that you are collecting stock options worth millions. Any sole proprietor is entitled to as much money he can amass for his hard work, but corporations should limit salaries and fringe benefits to $250,000 for all workers. That's enough money to live a comfortable life, educate your kids, and have some leftovers to share. This would be a great way to balance the federal budget. If corporations could only deduct $250,000 per worker as a cost of doing business, we would have large corporations sharing the tax burden.

Finally, it is wrong and a waste of your time to seek revenge. God has a plan in place to cover all contingencies. I will be including some lists of the possible plans he has developed for the revenge part of our existence at the end of this book.

I just noticed that I have covered a few of the Ten Commandments in nonprofessional terms quite by accident. There is a common thread that exists in the messages we see in all religions.

Being the outspoken person that I am, "out of necessity," I want to comment on the highway problems we have in America. It is all because of the stupid speed limit signs. Instead of putting signs up that say 55 mph, the powers that be should turn to the teachings of Thomas Gray (1716-1771) who said, "The paths of glory lead but to the grave." Imagine seeing a sign that says "All roads lead to your grave, so go as fast as you want to get there." It might be good to put a picture of the Grim Reaper pointing with his finger for extra effect. Please be extra careful if you see some fool running across the highway with a dog chasing his ass.

Men, I have to repeat a slogan about women. "Treat them according to the way you would like your daughter, sister, wife, or mother treated by others." Ladies, I have nothing to say about men. We are either perfect or hopeless! However, you are part of the problem. Conduct yourselves like you are somebody's daughter, sister, wife, or mother; and we will put an end to infidelity and mental and physical abuse in our lives. I say this because of the countless stories that appear in the newspapers outlining the social trauma that erupts because people forget these simple rules. I love my wife enough to say that if another man can bring more happiness to her life, then I want her to find that happiness. After all, it is her life. I also believe that when we die, we die alone. There is no reason to think that we own another human being. "She's mine" is a precursor to violence that we do not need in our lives. Summing up my private thoughts, don't worry about where life takes you with respect to your chosen career. It will change over time. Save as much money as you can along the way so that you increase your options when adversity strikes. Work in harmony with your coworkers instead of competing. To accomplish more work, we could learn not to worry about who gets credit for an idea. Eventually, the truth will come out!

20

"Have any of you prophets figured out why I have you all here? Do you think your presence here is just an accident? I wasn't going to tell you this, but there is too much fighting going on between you. And I think if you understand what I did, you might be more civil to one another. This is my world and universe. I created it because I wanted some company. At first, I made a few mistakes and created a bunch of cave-dwelling, hairy-looking people. I also forgot to make them in different colors. You know, I was so impressed with the grass and trees being green that I finally figured that it would be nice to add some color to their makeup. I realized also that I had to give them some more intelligence to make their lives more interesting. If later, I was to create TVs, remote channel changers for the men, and computers for all, I knew that I was going to have to continue to improve the model. That's why I keep sending new children down to the earth to keep up with the changing technology. Retiring the older models just makes sense because they are confused by these new gadgets and worn out from coping over the years."

I remember the shock of finding a small dead "thing" down at the vacant lot, which we visited each day as kids. It was only about one and a half feet in length. At first glance, it appeared to be an animal. I thought it was a space alien because it did not look like any animal I had ever seen. This memory has remained an image because I did not reach a conclusion at the time, and it remained an unanswered question floating around in my mind. Years later, I finally understood that I had happened across a fetus of a small child that had been discarded in the trash. I started to think about the possibility of me being that child and all that I would have missed along the way, including the overlapping of my life with others whom I have come in contact with that have a vested interest in my life. My kids would never have been born, and all the good that they are doing in their lives and of their grandchildren and their efforts to improve the world would go down the drain. Rest in peace is my only thought. Someone has a debt to repay, and I have to mention that you cannot take a lawyer with you on your special day in court!

Another sad reminder of my early years relates to my introduction to the world of sex at age nine. I didn't quite understand the how or the why of the whole thing, but for some odd reason, a fat rabbinical student decided that he had to have me. I thought he looked cute with his round hat and Santa Claus beard and probably provoked him getting too close. He carried me to the back room of one of the local stores and proceeded to remove his belt; I decided that this was not going to be nice and called out for help. Fortunately, a store owner intervened and managed to calm him down before it got ugly. It left me less trustful of those people wearing those strange-looking black hats. In addition, it taught me that the clergy are not superhuman or special. They are capable of doing all human things that we normal humans do. He was supposed to be training to lead us toward redemption but instead gave in to lust. Don't get me wrong; I am not down on the Jewish faith because of this incident. I look at the track record of the Catholic and Protestant faiths and conclude that lust is a real powerful companion in our lives. Still, I get very nervous around people who wear robes or black clothes. One of my finer moments in life that counters this incident was meeting a Jewish man who taught me how to fish. He was a paratrooper from World War II, who took some time out of his busy life to share his love of the sport with a young man who didn't have the towel to dry behind his ears. His lessons have stayed with me all my life. Thanks, mister!

I pretty much played life by ear and made my own mistakes for which I am happy. At the same time, I am sad that I did not have a lot of good stuff to pass on to my children. I don't know if you can imagine never playing ball or going fishing with your father, but that pretty much describes my early youth. Dad wore a white shirt and tie every day of his life and never got involved in my activities. He was a gentleman's gentleman and never got his hands soiled doing any work around the house. His involvement in my projects was limited to looking under my car on his way to work and asking, "How's it going, Bud?" This was my nickname that he assigned to me, and in the twenty years that I lived in his presence, he never used my real name.

When I was raising my kids, I found that I had become a creature of habit and tried to lock out the children from my world by spending too much time on my music. I soon woke up and began to act like a real father. Unfortunately, the kids did not buy into the fishing thing! I failed also in my attempt to build them a wagon from scrap lumber I had in the garage. It turned out to be too big and slow. At least I tried, thanks mostly to my wife who provided the direction.

I remember my good decision of using reverse psychology on my son who was somewhat weak and poor at sports. I told him I was ashamed of his performance in a softball game. It hurt like hell to say it, and it made him cry, but it had the desired effect. He grew, out of spite, into a strong man, able to handle any emergency that will come his way. It has also made him a better father to his children than I could ever be. Who knew he would go on to help save lives in the Katrina disaster? God knew!

Fortunately, for my children, my wife made up for my shortcomings in many ways. She came from a more stable environment. She actually celebrated birthdays and shared gifts as she was growing up. As our children were growing, she made it a point to start each birthday by serving a waffle at breakfast with a little candle in it and ended the children's birthday with a special rocket-ship cake or other artfully designed cake for the kids. I even got one on my day!

Her specialty was always being there for the kids. We always talked about the need for one parent to be available to soothe the ruffled feathers if the other parent saw fit to discipline the children for any reason. I always tried to bring them up the old-fashioned way—cry if you are hurt, but not if you want something. I always felt it was important to prepare them for the next great depression, sort of make them tough, so the world would not roll over them. I always promised my kids that I would not be their friend, but I would always be their father. They still don't quite understand that relationship. This was in stark contrast to my childhood training. The cat o' nine tails hung in the kitchen and used as a general-purpose tool for all sorts of minor indiscretions. I did everything short of committing murder as a child, so I have many body parts that have memories of their own. Fortunately, the tail stripes faded over the years, but lessons were learned.

I grew up memorizing things like "Don't let the door hit you in the ass on the way out," or "Don't tell me your problems, just your accomplishments." School was always in session. Times sure have changed; now they have time-outs. I think this was developed by the lawyers, so if you were caught swatting your child on the rear end, it justified an instant lawsuit. At least, I learned the difference between right and wrong at an early age. I am concerned that the next generation will miss some important lessons.

My children managed, all on their own, to dislocate an arm, get two black eyes from playing pillow fights in the dark, break a nose, and generally make my life at the hospital a scary time, waiting for the authorities to arrest me for child abuse. Parents did not take the kids to the hospital when I was growing up. Usually, the police called the ambulance and drove you home afterward to face the music.

21

Jesus Christ, who has been listening intently to the Creator's words about the animals, jumps into the conversation and adds, "I'm with you 100 percent on that idea of a second life as an animal. After all, I am supposed to sit at your right hand while the man judging goes on and agree that it could get a little grim. Some of these mortals are bound to leave stains after you reveal some of their rewards." There is a final consensus from all in attendance that the Creator is a wise person as gentle applause fills in the background.

What do you get when you cross a Seventh-Day Adventist with a Catholic? The end result can either be a very wise child who has been to the other side of the mountain or a very confused kid.

There were no such things as babysitters in my life, so because of the mixed religion of my parents, I attended the one church on Saturday and the other one on Sunday. I was always trying to figure out whether it was better to be a good Protestant or a bad Catholic. It was a little difficult to understand why the people washed one another's feet in one church, but not in the other. They spoke English in the one place and Latin in the other, but it turned out that they had one thing in common—they both had an offering to the church. I passed the collection plate at the Protestant service; but they had trusted elders, with stern faces, at the Catholic service who handled the money. I have to give it to the Catholic religion for marketing expertise. They started selling special masses for the dead. If you purchased a mass card, your sick or departed loved one could have their name mentioned in the mass, and the congregation would pray for their souls. I guess the poor and those without family and friends are up the creek.

Good deeds have gone on for time immemorial, performed by ordinary people like you and me. I get a little angry at the houses of worship and corporations that have a tendency to take credit for the good things that people do by having you belong to their group. Man's humanity to man is built inside of you, and it can come out on a daily basis. The houses of worship have claimed credit to our lives from birth to marriage to death. People actually go to college to learn how to reference the scriptures by number—special numbered verses at baptism, others at the weddings, and then some final numbered verses for your final exit. It seems like a moneymaking scheme is built around the need for closure in our lives. Keep your faith in a higher power of your choice, but leave your cash at home. You can't buy your way into heaven, but your faith will help sustain you in the troubled years you have ahead.

Mom did the duty of taking me to both places of worship even though her heart was not in it. Pop always slept in. He was an altar boy in his youth but lost something along the way. The story I heard was that his younger sister dropped dead in front of him when he was about twenty-five years of age. She hit the floor with a thud. It was instantaneous, without warning, and no amount of coaxing could bring her back. It must have been her time to go, and it had a profound effect on my father.

Back in the '40s, the Catholic teachings had to be the dominant religion for the offspring in a mixed marriage. The Protestants had to sign an agreement in writing that they would bring the children up in the Catholic religion. In addition, the Catholic cemetery was off-limits to the Protestants. You could not be buried with the person you shared your love with all your married life. Talk about rubbing salt in a wound. My mom did not complain about things too often, but living under these rules routinely gave her a bad taste for the Catholic religion. If you are going to be in the big picture puzzle with your neighbors, why is it wrong to lie with them in a graveyard? Who's making the rules here?

It is amazing to me how much church law has changed over the years; it was once a mortal sin to visit another person's church. Now it is encouraged. I also have a vivid picture in my head of a mother opening the door to the Sunday Catholic catechism class and handing her child to the big nun who was teaching God's love. She thanked the mother for making sure her son attended and closed the door. The nun then proceeded to punch and smack the child across the head eight or ten times before depositing him in the front row and advised him to never skip another class. Shocked by the incident, he couldn't or was afraid to cry. I wonder where and what she is today. Never mind, I do not want to know.

My strange religious training paid off for me in the long run as the only way you could get away from the barracks in boot camp was to attend church service. I had a good voice back then, and I can remember the choir director asking how many of the recruits were Baptists, Methodists, etc. I never raised my hand because one, that is a very dumb thing to do in boot camp; and two, I wasn't sure if I was still a legal Catholic. Either way, I got to sing lead during the later services and missed having to hang out at the shoe-shining affairs at the camp. I really loved those Protestant songs.

Years later, I worked for a Protestant veterinarian for a short time. He would call me into surgery and tell me that a Catholic cat had died from a shot he gave to end its suffering and that I would have to give the cat a proper Catholic burial at the landfill. I wrestled with this for a long time as I kept thinking about my old friend the neighborhood veteran, only I had to do it sober. Strange that people can make life decisions for their animals, but not themselves.

The veterinarian went on to become a full-bird colonel in the air force, and I will be forever grateful for the chats we had concerning my development. He was a truly sharing person who gave me some great advice when I needed it most. To this day, I am sorry for losing his son's snake that he brought to the office. Unbelievably, it was an accident that the snake went down the sink and got lost in the pipe. I was playing with him, trying to do some relationship building to get over my hang-ups, and he took off and headed right down the sink.

The doctor of veterinary medicine got even with me though. We had an incident at one of the warehouses on base when a pit viper got loose. He sent me on an assignment to go collect him and bring it to the clinic for identification. No amount of talking could convince him that he had picked the wrong man for the job. I went on the assignment and picked up the snake. However, its head was missing. I told the warehouse worker that it was hard to identify what kind of snake it was without seeing the head. He commented that it was very hard to kill it without smashing off its head. I collected the snake and brought it back to the doctor. He picked it up, examined it, and advised that it was just a common brown snake. In my mind, there was nothing common about it. It just brought back some old memories that I did not need to revisit. Back I went to the landfill for a proper burial.

22

"*While I was creating my world, I realized that the people would need some leaders, so I created each of you in my likeness and gave you some ability to wow the audience with my powers. Jesus, say hello to your brothers and sisters. Abraham, please hug your brother Muhammad.*

"*Now I know each of you thinks that you represent a special religious group and that your ideas are special, but that's not the case. The common thread of decency for your fellow man that exists in all religions was my message I sent with you on your journey. Somewhere along the line, fabricated religion took over and changed you into something that I do not recognize. I sent you down to mingle and give direction, but if you will notice, I have you all back again. I have since restricted all of you to this beautiful place as a reward for your sacrifices in my name.*

"*The trail of your deeds on earth has many people confused because stakeholders who recorded your movements to suit their needs have altered the stories along the way. There are at least six different scriptures that people are trying to live by, based on their early religious training. Lately, people have been showing up on their judgment day saying that their leaders made them do it. They are shocked when I tell them I am the only one who can turn them into a slug. Their religious leaders cannot because they do not share my power. I am Almighty God, and my powers are unlimited. If you think a drunken sailor is good at spreading around his assets, just wait until you see some of my tricks. I have a particularly fun time when some of the clergy, ministers, and religious nuts show up for their day in court. They all seem to have a surprised look and use the expression 'Say what?' when I tell them of their rewards for messing with my children. Jesus, do you remember the person who ordered your crucifixion? I fixed him good. I made a special glass cage for him to spend his eternity in until I get over my anger.*"

I have given up trying to be rich and famous. I have worked all my life just to pay bills, and the lottery thing has not worked. Being famous is intended for those very few people who arrived on earth with special talents. The burden these people carry is costly and often lonely. They can expect to lead very different lives from normal people. There are many copycats out there, but there are only a few special people with extraordinary gifts. There is only one great singer, one great piano player, and one great leader. It is a folly to try to be an imitation of the originals. I think it was part of the master plan to just put those special people here so we would have something to enjoy and emulate. "Angels in disguise!" I have been fortunate to meet some of these nice people who have made my life better.

So for the rest of us, we are presented with at least four real problems: (1) looking good in the eyes of our children (but be careful, for they can spot a phony and see through your cover-ups), (2) paying our dues as we consume the riches of this great earth, (3) chipping away at the evil we find as we grow old, and (4) getting ready for our future day in court.

Everything you do or say in the presence of your children is taken in and digested by them and serves as a reference point for all the future decisions that they make in life. They may not acknowledge things when they happen, but the children remember most of your indiscretions. All your actions will affect the outcome of history in one way or another. So when you wonder how the children will turn out, you can only turn to your memory of the lessons you taught. The image and reflection in our children's eyes are real.

Conservation is a big word and deserves mention only because the world is full of givers and takers. Every time you flip a switch to gain some comfort, you are consuming and taking. Make sure that you pay attention to the cost of your actions.

Many years ago, my wife approached me with the idea of creating a new doll to celebrate the bicentennial. We settled on the theme of an energy conservation doll that we could use to promote energy conservation for young children. She designed a doll and named it Shocka. I pointed out that he was a male doll and that we really needed a woman to get the message out to the children. This led to the birth of Momma Bulba. "Why stop there?" I asked, and she went on to design the rest of the Bulba Family—Energene, Electricia, and Little Kilo. Each of the dolls had hands, feet, and heads made in the shape of light bulbs. Everyone thought that it was a cute project and encouraged us to promote the idea. We spent all our savings trying to get the government to support the idea. However, trying to show the government a solution is impossible. We found that the energy-delivery companies did not want to conserve energy because they were in the business of selling their products, and the budgets approved for national conservation wasted on the bureaucracy. The project was not a total loss as it turned out to be one of the most enjoyable parts of our married life. Working with your spouse on a common project has many rewards.

On the subject of evil, I met the Grim Reaper face-to-face in the recovery room at the local hospital. I had an aneurysm on the night of the Columbine High School tragedy here in Colorado. They had so many students in for surgery that night that I had to move to a new room two times to accommodate the traffic. The funny thing was that he was not the grim-faced image that you would expect. The son of a bitch was smiling, which turned out to be the unnerving part of the encounter. He hung around for two days and left when I gave him the finger.

The future interview that we all must attend alone is probably the biggest problem we have to overcome. I can't emphasize too much the ticking clock and the chance you have in your hand. Some of us are going to experience a knee-bending, commode-hugging time when we meet the Big Guy! After you have done your time as an animal, you are relieved to get a work assignment in your third life. Morale is high in heaven as the slide straight to hell is quick if you screw up or complain. It's a perfect system! The clouds are used to hide the whiners that disappear on the spot. The lightning bolts that you see all around you are really energy trails showing where the souls entered the ground on their journey to the place that you don't want to go!

23

I wonder if God parties with his friends. Most of us think nothing of having a few drinks with our friends. But can you imagine God with a hangover? If he gets up one morning and forgets to check on the orbital path of the sun, we could all become crispy critters in an instant. Since the sun sets in the west, it makes sense to live as far west as possible in case he sobers up and gets back to work. I wonder if this is a literal interpretation of the passage in the Bible where it says we will be destroyed by fire. Look what happened when God left the water running the last time. Noah became an instant hero!

Have you done any thinking about the master plan? Most corporations and large businesses are studies in how things can go wrong. But spend a minute thinking about how really complex and well-organized life can be. Everything is covered. We have tears for those times when things are sad and laughter for the happy times, water when we are thirsty and snow for the skiers. Who thought of all these minute details? The organization of the place we refer to as Earth is amazing. Just recently, I learned that scientists have discovered the possibility of a negative universe. Therefore, I may have to revise my new church doctrine. If we do have a mirror image of life and earth in reverse, does that mean that we have to come back and relive our lives as the reverse of our current lives, where slaves come back as slave masters, before or after we come back as an animal? Something resembling a purgatory-holding zone, where Jews come back as Arabs and Catholics come back as Protestants? Are the gods playing games again? Makes sense to skip purgatory. Stop fighting with one another!

What would you do if the powers that be declared that starting at the end of this month, you could no longer refer to yourself as black or yellow or white and that you had to forget that you were Irish, Polish, Jewish, Russian, Japanese, etc.? Would you breathe a sigh of relief, raise your voice in anger, or set off a bomb? Think about your heritage, and tell me that you are not carrying a lot of extra unnecessary baggage. I gave up being Irish, except for one day a year, and saved a fortune on booze. Do you always have to be Egyptian, Israeli, American, Mexican, French, Indian, etc., and spend the rest of your life doing ritual things associated with your past heritage? Every bloodline carries with it an identity that must be preserved and carried to the next generation. That little bit of education causes most of the problems in our lives. Keep your family name free from dishonor, and honor the memory of those ancestors whose seed you carry into the next generation, but lose the extra baggage.

Our ancestors have all passed on to their just rewards and unpaid expenses for the bad things they did. Try living the rest of your short life just as yourself, unplugged and uncovered. We are all Muhammad's, Jesus Christ's, Gautama's, Abraham's, or Guru Nanak's disciples or followers of Hinduism or other religions. We just do not know who is on call duty each day. I believe that they operate much like doctors' offices in that they take days off and cover for one another. Therefore, we can never be sure who is there. What if you have been backing the wrong horse all these years? Would your beliefs be different if you were born in a different part of the world? Was it really your choice? For those who belong to a special religious group that practices sharing or trading only with fellow parishioners, remember the sun, moon, and stars given to us as a lesson in sharing—without strings!

Please get rid of that dumb-looking hat; it brings back memories of the fat rabbinical student I ran into as a child. If you don't like pain, then stop trying to announce to the world that you are special. We are all the same, onetime visitors to a planet we call Earth. We have turbans, feathers, robes and leather jackets, tattoos, motorcycles, special cars with fancy chrome wheels, expensive watches and jewelry, perfume, and small hats that we must wear in churches and synagogues—all special status symbols that make your neighbors uneasy. The color of your skin is not important, a badge of honor declaring "I am better than you are." We are all grains of sand blowing around in the universe. When you clump together with your own race, you take on the identity of the group and tend to scare people. Go along in life as a single nongroupie who has a purpose. Find why you were born into this world. When it comes time to bring out the old photo album and your kids say "These are my parents," are they going to be proud, or will you appear to look stupid?

Do you rebel against the pressures of life as a way of crying out for help? Many people refuse to be classified as a grain of sand and will do anything to stand out and appear special. They will disrupt the system and rebel against authority as much as possible because they are alone and lost. Crybabies to be sure, but they need help.

If you are able to look at the substance abuse picture closely, you will see weak, lost people who do not know how to cope. Surprise, we all fall down and get bruises along the way. The secret is to get up and try again. I don't want you to feel that I am not a believer in a higher power because I spoke with my maker one on one and came away impressed with the peace I got from the encounter. I go back often for chats. By the way, he does not have a fax or an e-mail address, and it is not necessary to seek him out in one of those expensive religious places. Just look him or her up directly in the quiet of your room.

I am getting a little nervous about how I am going to react if my theory holds true about the reincarnation stuff and people start genuflecting when they approach me. One year, I let my beard grow, and I scared the hell out of one person who thought Jesus had come back. Please promise me, no bowing.

Some of the early religious leaders must have been athletic by nature and passed on exercise lessons at prayer time. We have people all over the world bowing and kissing the ground and walls and using hand gestures in secret code. Come on, people, religious wars and rituals should have ended in the Middle Ages. This is the new millennium, and it's time to grow up and come into the light. You are a child of the Almighty God and should act accordingly.

Can someone please tell me how it is possible for a man to be highly educated, speak ten or more languages, and then allow people to come and kiss his ring? Workers like you and me paid for him to sit on his duff and read books so he could have a free ride. He is surrounded by legions of robe-wearing lesser-titled assistants, who also aspire to a free meal at the expense of others. Mr. Pope, it is time to get off your butt and do something about truth and sharing. Sell some or all the assets of the church, feed the poor, and try to end some of the suffering in people's lives by helping to locate, uncover, and criticize the extremists who do not improve life on earth. Do not spend any more time researching and canonizing saints. Their saintly acts have already earned them a place in the big night sky.

I do not mean to single out the pope and blame him for all the world's problems; all the other religious leaders are just as guilty of inaction and should be held accountable. My familiar connection to Catholicism made me think of the Vatican first, but there are many palaces and temples around the world.

In defense of our last pope, I have to say that he made a good attempt to contact the other religious leaders to apologize for his religious heritage. This was a first and good attempt to show the world that we are all brothers and sisters.

If I wind up opening a church, anyone over sixteen can sit quietly in comfort, smoke if he wants in the seats on the left, and leave the kids outside to build an old-fashioned bonfire. Be sure to leave them a few (blank) bullets and a potato or two so they will be really impressed and educated when you get back. Tithing will be limited to 1 percent, a full 9 percent below the going rate, so the rich will not gain an unfair advantage. No names will be published showing the amount of your contribution. No charge if you are out of work. Your contributions will cover administrative costs and an occasional steak and dish of ice cream for your new leader. I refuse to wear a fancy robe and will be dressed in slacks and a comfortable shirt with no hat if you go looking for me.

I have learned a lot over the years about houses of worship. Churches are built with your money, on a new vacant land near the newest housing development. The banks and the churches compete for the best location in our neighborhoods, along with your finances. The churches are richly adorned and have the finest public speakers that have memorized all the critical passages in the books by number. All designed to solicit more money from you so they don't have to get a real job. Let us put some fun in their lives by stopping all monetary contributions to their cause for a period of six months. I will bet they come out of the woodwork like cockroaches after you. Now there is an idea for a next life.

I tried to enroll my boys in the Boy Scout troupe that was being run by one of the Protestant church groups in the area and was greeted by a silken-handed pastor who advised that we were welcome to join as long as we understood the local policy of tithing 10 percent to cover expenses. I thought it through and decided that any man with a weak handshake that felt like a dead fish was not worthy of trusting to look out for my children's welfare. I think he needs to get a job and stop living off the hard work of others.

For all of us, it is time to take responsibility for our way of life. We are capable of change. The opportunity to make this a better world is in our hands. What do we have to do to make sure that history never repeats itself?

Where are all the living religious leaders these days? Few, if any, have stood up and said, "Stop the killing," "Hug your enemy," or at least "Help the poor bastard." The world has become too political. All the religious writings that have been around for years are full of inspirational messages that the leaders should be using at this time to put an end to the bad karma that is going around the world. Any ayatollahs or holy men, get the word from your gods, and please stand up and make your presence known!

24

"I have since decided to put a little piece of myself into each of the mortals over at the DNA vat, with the hope that they will listen to the little voice inside them that will lead them back into my kingdom. I also gave them another voice to follow if they want to branch out on their own and suffer the consequences for being a thankless child. I know this comes as a shock to some of you prophets, but I have many children, none more important than the other. I love you all, but I would be a much happier creator if you would stop the fighting."

For sure, my attempt to save the world will fail. However, I have discovered that sometimes, just being in the presence of certain people has a profound effect on people's lives. There are many good people on earth that you encounter each day. On close inspection, you will find the group is composed of past sinners seeking redemption, along with true sharing people who work tirelessly without compensation to improve the lives of strangers. This is in sharp contrast to the groups that seek publicity and payment or stipends for their efforts. The sharing group encourages me to speak to all of you out there who are discouraged that you have not had a profound influence on the world.

Thomas Gray used a line in his writings that said, "Full many a gem of purest ray serene / The dark unfathomed caves of ocean bear / Full many a flower is born to blush unseen / And waste its sweetness on the desert air." When I hear those words, I envision a small child standing in a dark slum window, with the sun setting, and two little shining gems of tears staring back at me. I would like to invite you to the party of life. Draw a circle around your life, and help those who are in your circle. Everyone you meet on a daily basis, all your puzzle-piece neighbors should be in your circle. Even the person with the Help Me sign qualifies for consideration. Stop and talk with him. You can't save the world either. However, you can surely effect change all around you.

"When you see misery, give it all you have, even if it's only a tear," as Thomas would say. If you see injustice and hate in your circle, speak up and stop it. If you see hunger, feed it. Share your entire God-given gifts with those who step into your circle. Once the idea catches on, we will see interlocking circles built on the concept of love, and then you can say that you did your part even if it is a small part that you play in helping a neighbor or coworker cope with life and their black clouds. If you find your reason for being on this earth, you may not turn out to be great or famous in the eyes of the world, but you will shine in the darkest of places. The shine will be especially noticeable in the mirror that you look at on a daily basis. You will start to like what you see. It might be helpful for prison authorities to understand this connection. If then, the prisoners could realize that they are children of God—and not second-class inferior citizens; we might make some progress in repairing our costly and wasteful prison systems.

The beauty of this plan is there are no donations for overhead or salaries and administration. No advertising or mass mailings have to be used to raise money. You do not have to participate in any walkathons, bikeathons, or running events. You just help your neighboring puzzle piece in your daily contact circle. The important thing to remember is that your circle will keep changing as you live your life. If you like to travel, your influence will be felt all over the world.

Can you imagine the possibilities that would present themselves if you adopted some of my advice? White men could walk in Harlem without fear. Jews could walk the streets of Palestine waving to his neighbors with a smile. You could talk to the person sitting next to you on a bus or subway without fear of reprisal. You could really feel good about yourself and how you fit into the big picture. It is unfortunate I will not be around to experience most of what I speak about, for my time is growing short. This is not a sad thing or something that makes me feel bad because I am looking forward to the new challenges in my second life. If you consider your life and can imagine it without drugs and violence, you can attain it through small changes in your daily lifestyle.

It took a very long time for me to find one of my reasons for being. It is a small one, but it qualifies because it is something I can leave behind for my fellow man. I received no compensation for my efforts, and some future citizen might live an extra day because of my taking an interest.

Traveling to work each day along Highway 6 in Golden is a little dangerous. There are only two places along this two-lane winding mountain road where it is relatively safe to pass. If all drivers could travel the length of this road at forty miles per hour, there would be no need to pass. Unfortunately, the speed signs fluctuate between thirty and forty-five miles per hour, creating backup when law-abiding drivers heed the signs. This tends to make you look forward with enthusiasm to the two passing zones. The road broadens to three lanes, and since everyone is waiting to use them, it takes on the resemblance of the finish line at the Daytona Speedway. I competed with everyone else on the way up the mountain and never gave it much thought; but one day, on the way down, I noticed that the three lanes were really sharing lanes for traffic going in both directions. The one broken line on the way down the hill encouraged drivers to head in to the stock-car derby coming up the canyon. To make a long story short, I contacted the highway authorities and convinced them to make a change. Highway marker 263.5 now has a solid line on the side coming down the hill. Some unknown neighbor of mine now gets to live another day because I passed this way. Yeah!

I had hoped that they would put up a small plastic sign attesting to the fact that I had passed this way on my journey through the universe, but considering all the black clouds and rain that might show up, I think the highway authorities thought better of the idea. In any event, I am busy trying to get them to change speed-limit signs. Wish me luck!

I remember my earlier years, driving back and forth to college, and the daily sight of seeing a group of poor disabled people walking hand in hand together down the street. After a while, I found it fairly depressing to watch them and looked for other streets to travel so I could get to class. This is another example of the bad mistakes I made in life that I cannot take back. I was ashamed of my actions, and their image kept haunting me. I came to realize that these people were just trying to cope with their less-than-fortunate circumstances, and they were helping one another along by holding hands so none would get lost or fall. I did not learn this lesson in class, but rather from a group of people whose mission in life may have been to teach us this lesson. I used the incident to develop a fund-raising script for charities, surrounding the concept of holding hands with your neighbors. I still can't deal or cope with that degree of suffering because it just makes a basket case out of me, which is not good to show to those involved. I offer my gratitude to those who can cope and who volunteer to help. They have a special gift of being able to interface on a one-on-one basis. I have learned that I can only help from afar with monetary contributions and fundraising for select nonreligious groups.

25

I have not talked much about rainbows and the pot of gold, but I have found them. One of the lessons taught by my father was to always protect and bring honor to the family name. That has served as a helping model as I've dealt with the decisions about what is right or wrong.

The neighborhood police officer is actually your friend and helps to remind you that life is not free. Every act costs something. So the family name is preserved and passed on to my sons for safekeeping. My daughter threw hers away and took another name when she got married, but the same rules apply. Each has brought honor in their own way to their ancestors. That is the only reward a parent can reap for their years of dedication and hard work. That's another great secret: you can never pay back your parents. You can only invest in your children, or in humankind, by using the good lessons taught by your parents.

For the orphans of the world, you were dealt a different hand, and your road will be a little rougher. It won't be as bad as the small fetus that I found in the vacant lot, and if you trust in your neighbor, you will find some special people out there who will share. You are a child of the universe who has a purpose! Looking on the bright side of things, you will get to skip some of the tasks my children have ahead of them, including making decisions to commit their parents to a nursing home, supplementing their social security—budget lifestyle, cleaning out sixty years of souvenirs, and carrying a heavy box to the cemetery. Not something you look forward to doing, but this is life's plan.

I keep thinking of visiting my ancestral home in a small town called Kilkenny, Ireland, in the county of Cork. I heard from a merchant seaman, who had grown up in Ireland and traveled the country extensively, that the town was the home of the Kilkenny Hellcats. The story went that if they couldn't find someone to fight, they would pick a fight with one another. Maybe this is where I got my bold fighting spirit to never give in to adversity.

I am saddened that the Irish have never been able to accommodate more than one religion in their borders. The old Irish songs don't speak of hatred for one another. Maybe it is time to listen to the real heart of the Irish. You can appreciate what a problem it would be for me to stand in the middle of Ireland with my split religious background and not know whether to wear green or orange clothing.

I guess I lied earlier when I said there would not be any more poetry. I'm still refining one about nature, but it is too early to share. There is a certain amount of beauty in nature that we miss when we live our busy lives. During my last layoff, I didn't think about cashing in my chips; instead, I used the time for quiet reflection. We had a little robin's nest on our back porch, and I had the luck to catch the first day of flight for four baby robins. Three of them just jumped out without giving it a thought, but one of them was not quite sure. The mother and father robin took up positions about ten feet from the nest and encouraged the baby by chirping and calling in robin talk that it was time to go. It was a great feeling to see the little guy spread his wings and fly. It is equivalent to the final payoff that parents receive when they see their children standing on their own two feet and coping.

I recall another incident that had to do with our pups that were experiencing their first exposure to snow. Brother and sister from the same litter (Reuben and Chelsea) took up a position on the porch and sat quietly next to each other, observing this newfound wonderland in the backyard. It was a special scene that I had the fortune to see and will write about when I find the proper words. The two dogs were a gift given to my wife and me after our loyal companion, Dreyfus, passed on. It was difficult to adjust to the idea of replacements for our family member who grew up with the children and had a personality all his own. This will serve as my official thank-you to the kids for their efforts as the replacements turned out to be another rainbow in our lives. Imagine that, actually learning something from your children. That's new!

I would be remiss if I did not mention Lefty. She was a local squirrel who showed up at our back door each day, looking for some food. My wife, who noticed that her front left paw was missing, gave her the name Lefty. The impressive thing about Lefty was her ability to scramble up a tree and get away from Reuben and Chelsea, who had established turf boundaries that could never be violated.

Somehow, this little squirrel got around her disability and learned to fully function in the wild. On close inspection, it appeared she stepped on a live electrical connection and burned her limb off at the elbow. It took about six months of training, but I finally convinced her to eat out of my hand instead of eating my hand. Finally, I was permitted to pet her head; and when I pet her back, she would completely relax her tail and lay it flat on the ground.

She repaid me by getting pregnant and having a litter of five offspring in my attic. You have probably never seen a two-inch baby squirrel, but boy, are they cute. I kept thinking about how cute they were as I repaired my fireplace from the damage of having them as guests. I believe her lessons on coping were inspirational to my wife who developed multiple sclerosis in her late forties. She applies Lefty's lessons on a daily basis to help her get through the bad days.

Nature teaches great lessons if we pause to smell the roses. Pets add a new dimension to our lives that we cannot anticipate. When our dog Reuben started into his second year, certain traits from his first life started to show through. He had to have been a thief! Every now and then, he would disappear into another room; and we would find him hunting through the trash pails, clothing, or anything that looked intriguing. We came home one day and found that he took it upon himself to rifle into a five-pound bag of potatoes that had been left on a countertop. He didn't try to eat them; instead, he carefully carried them one by one and placed them behind each chair at the dining room table. I think he was trying to help set the table. We gave up trying to change his habits and instead enjoyed the variety and joy he brought to our lives.

My real blessing, and the pot of gold everyone looks for, came to me in the form of an ability to feel what the great musicians of our world are experiencing when they perform. As an example, most people would gloss over the four notes that Louis Armstrong played as he started his solo in the tune "Dippermouth Blues." When I hear them, shivers go down my spine. He uses the four notes to announce that it's time to clear the decks. "Here comes Louie, and I have something to say." His spirit will echo into the next few generations. How about yours?

Many years ago, I happened into a small bar in Cape Cod, Massachusetts, that was a local hangout during the summer months for many of the college students from Boston. Sitting at an old upright piano was a woman called Gladys, whom I cannot get out of my mind. She was playing upbeat rowdy songs in the club, best described as a watering hole, with a noisy, inattentive crowd. I noticed that she had passed a beer glass to a table filled with students drinking a pitcher of beer. They passed a one-fourth-filled glass of beer back to the piano for Gladys. I decided that she was entitled to a fresh beer because she was in my circle, and it was not a big deal, just a random act of kindness. I instructed the waiter to send her a bottle. She turned to look at me when the beer was delivered and at break time, visited my table. She explained that she did not drink and was simply passing her glass to the students to collect money for her favorite charity. She explained that the boys were being rude by putting beer in her glass. I took this charity explanation with a grain of salt because Gladys was in her seventies, and I thought she was supplementing her pension. This was another one of my big mistakes. Our friendship developed as I continued to visit the hangout on a weekly basis over the summer. One night, she said that I should visit the other place that she played at on Tuesday evenings, a restaurant that used background piano music and not as loud as the other place. I made the trip one Tuesday and walked into one of the most enjoyable nights of my life. There was Gladys sitting at a concert grand piano, playing flawless music from memory, with a smile on her face that said welcome. I can still see the twinkle in her eyes. She explained that she was a music consultant to Radcliffe College and did this to keep young. At the end of the summer season, I passed her an envelope with twenty dollars to thank her for making my summer something special. Two weeks later, I received the money back, with a special thank-you from Gladys for her fun summer. She invited me to stop by and visit her in the Boston area during the off-season. I should have known by the name of the address she gave me that I was out of my league, but I attempted to visit. I found myself pulling up to an expensive-looking house in Knob Hill, Boston, and I was surprised to find that she had a professional butler decked out in a tuxedo. He greeted me and advised she was not at home. Unfortunately, I was unable to return as I transferred to another base shortly afterward. That ended my relationship with Gladys, but the memory lingers on. I have learned the great lesson of never judging a book by its cover. Life is full of people like Gladys sprinkled all around us, and they have tremendous gifts to share. Some of them might even be your neighbors.

26

"I'm impressed with your power and plans, Big Guy, but can we get back to the puzzle for a minute? How will we know when the puzzle is complete?" asks Gautama.

"Why do you ask? Do you have a date or something? Are you going somewhere I don't know about? Now settle down. This is going to be fun," says the Creator. "I am going to light up the sky each night with bright stars so you can see how much progress you are making with the picture."

"I really want the Second Coming to be special, so all of you prophets had better start planning now. Instead of just sending one representative, I have elected to send all of you on this trip. You can all figure on being really busy with your followers. After you arrive, the e-mails should fly, trying to find out where you are holding your meetings. Most of the people you meet will speak the words 'I'm sorry.' All of them will be on their knees, some for the first time, realizing that this is a serious situation. Those that have a lot to lose will begin to plot your assassinations, so be careful out there. All the churches will probably post Welcome signs and gather all the important leaders together and have a special collection. In short, all hell is going to break loose. The whole idea is too shocking to imagine. I guess it would be good for the world to experience the years that lead up to your visits where the way is prepared first with peace and kindness by following the water jug carrier."

Purposely, I have left some blank spots on the charts that follow so you can fill it in yourself. Use the brain that your god gave you, and use some imagination. I have not worked out all the bugs yet on this church-doctrine stuff, like for how long is your sentence and what happens if someone shoots you on a hunting trip. I will get back to you. Whatever you do, don't kill the snakes or step on the spiders. They are doing their penance and should live extra long lives.

I have come to realize that there are three kinds of people in this world—normal ones like you and your next-door neighbor, predators, and me.

The trouble is finding out too late who's who. For a long while, I questioned why God saw it fit to make both kinds of animals, the truly gentle fawn and the ferocious predatory lion. The answer came to me at the zoo, and I'm not going back.

There is some really bad stuff going on in our lives. Everyone has to pay for breaking the rules. Jail time is nothing compared to the final rewards you will reap for living your life in less-than-a-kind way. Chill out, and start thinking about becoming a believer in my solutions to the world's problems. Preach peace, and demonstrate love to your neighbors. I am really looking forward to coming back as a big brown bear, roaming the hillsides, fishing (I love fishing) in spring, and sleeping all winter. I also realize that I can come back as a white-colored bear and live in a very cold place. Based on my luck up to this point, it could go either way.

I forgot to tell you that I did put a note in the box I sent home to my parents. I was afraid it would get lost if I laid it on top, so I put it in the pants pocket. I wasn't smart enough to say, "Thanks, Mom and Dad, for all your hard work"; but I did give them my new address, hopeful that they would write and help end the loneliness.

Unless you haven't guessed by now, I am a sinner! I want to go on record and say that I am not perfect in any way and have many memories of past mistakes that I would like to forget. The world is less than perfect, so I am right at home. The earth is full of people who are dysfunctional and come from broken homes and marriages. Some have a good education, and others barely get along without the ability to read. Add in those that have some form of mental or physical disability. Stir in the rich and poor and the highly educated. Sprinkle in the superior-minded moral churchgoing crowd who will not acknowledge your existence unless you tithe to their church group, along with the religious fanatics who go around blowing things up. Then blend in the good people already on the earth, and you have a small idea of how difficult it would be to solve the world's problems. There are actually some people out there who could care less about anybody or anything, adopting a fainéant attitude toward life. They are usually rich or well-off and think they are having the time of their lives. They have made steady progress in their chosen career field and measure their success by the size of their bank accounts. I see them all the time, riding along the highway with the top down on their new convertibles, usually with a big smile on their face as they pass and pay no attention to the man standing with the sign that says Will Work for Food.

The world is a lonely place to be on your own. Make some friends through sharing, and the journey becomes interesting and rewarding. Trust me on this—you are a onetime visitor like me, with two lives to go.

To my creator, I can only say, "Thanks, mister, for a fun trip! I'm still a lowly street urchin lost in your garden, but I am coming your way. It might be good to mention it to Guru Nanak as he and I have a few things to discuss." I have to make a stop-off first, mostly to pay for the biggest sins a man ever committed—shaving at the wrong time and leaving the toilet seat up. If you see me tiptoeing around the forest stepping over the snakes, don't shoot; I am doing my penance.

I thought about having a talk with God, asking why he can't be a more gentle, loving kind of guy and came to the conclusion that he put a little piece of himself in each of us for the purpose of letting us do the hard work developing into caring human beings! I finally understand the difference between a friend and a father.

If I do make it to heaven, I will be displaying my blue card (without a gold seal). Look for me cleaning the latrines near the pearly gates. I will not be complaining!

God's Revenge Chart

How bad have you been? I have made up a hypothetical chart showing the possible next-life continuances for offenders.

Types of Animal-Related Sins
alligator: corporate sneak baboon: liar cockroach: unethical salesperson crocodile: bad politician eel: religious leader on the take elephant: couch potato mouse: sex offender snake: murderer slug: lazy person spider: lawyer who defends guilty people for profit

Classification of Future Reverse-Image Assignment
Arab: Jew bully: wimp Catholic: Protestant Indian: Pakistani Irish Catholic: Irish Protestant Jew: Arab North Korean: South Korean white: black
Redeeming Acts: Time Off for Good Behavior
help a child: 5 years
charity to a neighbor: 5 years
hug your reverse-image partner: 15 years
listen to bad rap music: +2 years

Bibliography

BBC World Service. "Your Guide to Religions of the World." *http://www. bbc.co.uk/religion/religions/*.

Gershwin, George and Irving Caesar. "Swanee." 1988 *Déjà Vu: The Al Jolson Collection*. 5020-2 Phonographic Performance Ltd., Ganton House, 14-22 Ganton Street, London W1V 1LB.

Oliver, Joseph and Louis Armstrong. "Dippermouth Blues." *Heart Full of Rhythm*. Vol. II (GRD-620). With Jimmy Dorsey and his orchestra. Los Angeles, California: Edwin H. Morris & Company/MCA Publishing, a division of MCA, Inc., (ASCAP), 1936.

S9.Com: The Biographical Dictionary. "Goodman, Benjamin David (Benny)." U.S. jazz and swing bandleader, musician, and clarinetist (1909-1986). http://www.s9.com/Biography/Goodman-Benjamin-David.

S9.Com: The Biographical Dictionary. "Williams, John Towner." U.S. conductor and composer of *Jaws* music score (1975). http://www. s9.com/Biography/Williams-John-Towner.

Selections from the Poetry and Prose of Thomas Gray. Edited with an introduction and notes by William Lyon Phelps. The Athenaeum Press Series. Boston: Ginn & Company, 1894.

The Columbia World of Quotations 1996. "Quote 52001 by William Shakespeare." British dramatist, poet (1564-1616). Lear, in *King Lear*. Act 1, sc. 4, 1. 268-9 (1623). http://www.bartleby.com/66/1/52001.html.

Your Friends For Tomorrow—The Bulba Family (figurines). Designed by Ann C. Bolger (Copyright 1976). Used with permission.